Doris Ann Goodchild
May 1984

HERE & THERE WITH PEN & SKETCH PAD

"A double blessing is a double grace
Occasion smiles upon a second leave."
so said Polonius — W.S

© Doris Ann Goodchild 1984.

Cased & Limited Edition
Signed & Numbered
ISBN 0 947620 01 X
Paper back
ISBN 0 947620 00 1

AT HOME

ABROAD

For
M·M·B
who plotted & planned
many of these excursions
& who asked me
to write these pages;

& for
B·J·P·
who is unfailingly
encouraging
& full of good advice;

& for
M·J·R· & those friends
who so happily shared
in these modest ventures,

here is a collection of pages
which combine to make a small book
for dipping into from time to time,
page by page as mood & interest suggest.

WINDMILL
IN CRETE.

"In this moment there is life and food
For future years." W·W·

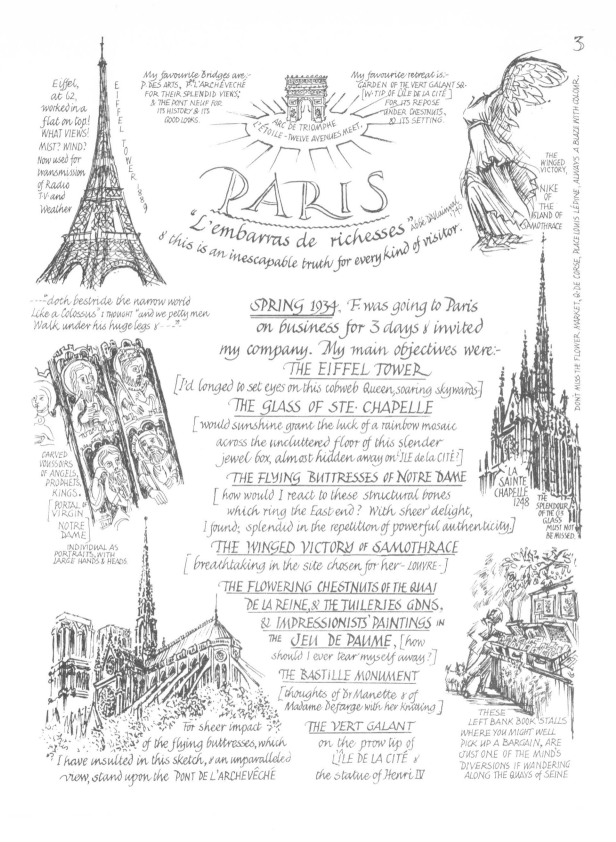

Eiffel, at 62, worked in a flat on top.! WHAT VIEWS! MIST? WIND? Now used for transmission of Radio T.V. and Weather

EIFFEL TOWER 1889

My favourite Bridges are:- P. DES ARTS, Pt. L'ARCHÉVECHÉ FOR THEIR SPLENDID VIEWS; & THE PONT NEUF FOR ITS HISTORY & ITS GOOD LOOKS.

ARC DE TRIOMPHE L'ÉTOILE - TWELVE AVENUES MEET.

My favourite retreat is:- GARDEN OF THE VERT GALANT SQ. [W. TIP OF L'ÎLE DE LA CITÉ FOR ITS REPOSE UNDER CHESTNUTS, & ITS SETTING.

THE WINGED VICTORY, NIKE OF THE ISLAND OF SAMOTHRACE

PARIS

"L'embarras de richesses" _Abbé D'Vainval 1740_

& this is an inescapable truth for every kind of visitor.

----"doth bestride the narrow world Like a Colossus" I THOUGHT "and we petty men Walk under his huge legs &---".

SPRING 1934, F. was going to Paris on business for 3 days & invited my company. My main objectives were:- THE EIFFEL TOWER [I'd longed to set eyes on this cobweb Queen, soaring skywards]

THE GLASS OF STE. CHAPELLE [would sunshine grant the luck of a rainbow mosaic across the uncluttered floor of this slender jewel box, almost hidden away on L'ÎLE de la CITÉ?]

THE FLYING BUTTRESSES OF NOTRE DAME [how would I react to these structural bones which ring the East end? With sheer delight, I found; splendid in the repetition of powerful authenticity.]

THE WINGED VICTORY & SAMOTHRACE [breathtaking in the site chosen for her - LOUVRE -]

THE FLOWERING CHESTNUTS OF THE QUAI DE LA REINE, & THE TUILERIES GDNS, & IMPRESSIONISTS' PAINTINGS IN THE JEU DE PAUME, [how should I ever tear myself away?]

THE BASTILLE MONUMENT [thoughts of Dr Manette & of Madame Defarge with her knitting]

THE VERT GALANT on the prow tip of L'ÎLE DE LA CITÉ & the statue of Henri IV

CARVED VOUSSOIRS OF ANGELS, PROPHETS, KINGS. [PORTAL OF VIRGIN NOTRE DAME] INDIVIDUAL AS PORTRAITS, WITH LARGE HANDS & HEADS.

For sheer impact of the flying buttresses, which I have insulted in this sketch, & an unparalleled view, stand upon the PONT DE L'ARCHÉVECHÉ

LA SAINTE CHAPELLE 1248

THE SPLENDOUR OF THE (13 GLASS MUST NOT BE MISSED.

DON'T MISS THE FLOWER MARKET, Q. DE CORSE, PLACE LOUIS LÉPINE, ALWAYS A BLAZE WITH COLOUR.

THESE LEFT BANK BOOK STALLS WHERE YOU MIGHT WELL PICK UP A BARGAIN, ARE JUST ONE OF THE MIND'S DIVERSIONS IF WANDERING ALONG THE QUAYS of SEINE

SUMMER 1946 I had wanted to be on the first Passenger Channel crossing after the war. Soon the chance came. My good friend B·R· ["the Frensh she spak ful faire and fetisly" as did Chaucer's Nun] & I, took leeward seats on deck & rocked our way over NEWHAVEN DIEPPE with blessings on this freedom of travel once again, after harrowing years of disquiet, apprehension, tragedy, [LONDON & BRISTOL FOR ME] & the grim confinement of blackout.

Paris, we knew, had suffered privation. We expected to eat frugally & walk everywhere — infrequent buses, few taxis, BUT GOOD LEGS NEVER FAILED!

Now for those grand Haussmann perspectives once again, to be seen from PLACE DE LA CONCORDE, ARC DU CARROUSEL — also from PONT DES ARTS, P. DE LA TOURNELLE etc

WITH A SENSE OF HEIGHTENED AWARENESS, ONE FEASTS THE EYES ON MAN'S ARCHITECTURAL ACHIEVEMENTS, AS IF FOR BOTH THE FIRST, & LAST, TIME.

Walk, wander, wonder. L'ÎLE DE LA CITÉ; LATIN QUARTER; FLOWER MARKETS; FLEA MARKETS; PRINTS; BISTROS; CHARCUTERIES; EPICERIES; GALLERIES; MUSEUMS.

Back streets; jostling houses, with mansard roofs; tall chimney stacks; hooded windows; flowery ironwork balconies; carved doors, Victor Hugo, de Musset, Balzac... Quayside book stalls; Faubourg St Germain [the C18 Nobility Quarter] & the high class shops round about la Madeleine.

"Sunday chicken in every pot."

HENRI IV SQUARE DU VERT GALANT ORIGINALLY ERECTED BY HENRI'S SON LOUIS XIII

ONE OF THE SEA HORSES OF FONTAINE de L'OBSERVATOIRE CARPEAUX, by FREMIER

THE CARACOLING HORSES ON PLINTH OF PONT ALEXANDRE III

LOUIS XIII BIRD FANCIER SON OF HENRI IV Place des Vosges

CHARIOT HORSES MOUNTED ABOVE ARC DU CARROUSEL TO CELEBRATE NAPOLEON'S VICTORIES 1805

SOME OF THE DOMES OF PARIS
PANTHÉON 1790
1029 CHURCH OF SORBONNE
THE INVALIDES 1735
SACRÉ COEUR

FIVE CLUSTERED LAMPS HÔTEL DE VILLE COUR DE MAI SEE ALSO CLUSTERED LAMPS PONT ALEXANDRE III AND MANY OTHERS.

"CHOCOLAT DANSANT DANS LE BAR D'ACHILLE." BY TOULOUSE LAUTREC THE WIZARD DRAUGHTSMAN. [MY APOLOGIES TO HIM.]

THE PONT NEUF CROSSES THE PROW, W. END OF BOAT SHAPED L'ÎLE DE LA CITÉ. SEE THE SPLENDID VIEW FROM PONT DES ARTS, SHOWING QUAI DE L'HORLOGE, Q. DES ORFEVRES, Q. DE CONTI, & VEDETTES FOR RIVER TOUR, SPIRES OF STE. CHAPELLE & NOTRE DAME

What a view! Photographed & drawn a thousand times. NOTE BRIDGE MASKS.

THE VIGOUR, VITALITY, & SPARKLE OF THE IMPRESSIONISTS, NEVER FAILS TO EXCITE ✻ ✻ THE CONTOURS & DESIGN OF DOMES, & THE MANY SCULPTURED HORSES OF PARIS WOULD MAKE ABSORBING STUDIES.

MONTMARTRE had to be explored. Utrillo, V.Gogh, Toulouse Lautrec & many other artists sprang to mind in this teeming Arts world.

THE COMÉDIE FRANÇAISE gave us:-
Molière: "Tartuffe" & "Le Médecin malgré lui"
De Musset: "On ne badine pas avec l'amour"
Jules Renard: "Poil de Carotte"
SEAT 1/8° + SERVICE, PROGRAMME 5° COFFEE 1/1

THE THÉÂTRE DE L'OPÉRA gave us:-
"La Flûte Enchantée" [CEILING SEAT 10°]
[THE OLD VIC – SEAT IN 'GODS' = 6°]
Four Ballets 3rd TIER BOX SEAT 1/8°

PARIS ITSELF IS A THEATRE, OF FREE SPECTACLES, OPEN FOR ALL TO SEE
"Men's eyes were made to look, and let them gaze" W.S.

DO SEE THE ENCHANTING TAPESTRIES CALLED "THE SENSES" IN THE
CLUNY MUSEUM

DO SEE INTRICATE IRONWORK OF THE WEST PORTAL NOTRE DAME

LE PETIT TRIANON

THE BOURBON PALACE OF VERSAILLES (17
11 mls S·W· of Paris, Louis [THE SUN KING] XIV built it as a retreat from life in Paris, at fantastic cost & lived in it with 1,000 noblemen. Louis XVI found The Petit Trianon [ordered by Louis XV & the retreat of Marie Antoinette] more to his taste. So do I!
[‘A CHACUN SON GOÛT’ or ‘chacun à son goût’]

One recalls "THE ADVENTURE" by Moberly & Jourdain relating their mysterious experiences in the garden 1901

WHAT PLAY ON THEME & VARIATIONS IN SCALE & TREATMENT OF BUD TENDRIL FLOWER LEAF ETC.

THIS DRAWING SHOWS BUT A SOUPÇON

THE CATHEDRAL OF CHARTRES
IN APRIL 1956,

we were bowling across the flat plain of the Beauce, my whole being agog for the slender sculptures & jewel like windows of the Cathedral. From afar we descried two needles, [like heralds-like cypresses] ⊥⊥ pricking the ruler flat 'desert' skyline. Isolated twin spires? We flew on, the car eating the miles. Later, bulk joined the 2 spires ⊥⊥ to be eventually skirted by the town itself.

Excitement raced as we approached the Royal Portal to study the glories of this Medieval Masterpiece. Minutes flew by in the spell of close contemplation. Hours were too short. "The conscious stone to beauty grew" wrote Emerson.

We took a picnic in the Museum Gdns, then walked along the River Eure to enjoy old houses & bridges.

"BEHOLD YE BUILDERS DEMI GODS" SAID WATTS DUNTON

PYTHAGORAS (6 BC

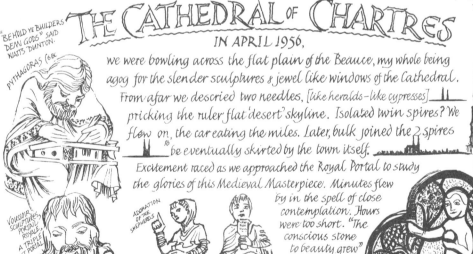

VOUSSOIR SCULPTURES, PORTAIL ROYALE, A TRIPLE WEST PORTAL

DONATUS OR ARISTOTLE (5th/12
PORTAIL ROYALE

ADORATION OF THE SHEPHERDS.

WEST FRONT CHARTRES CATH· TOWER SPIRES NOT TWINS NORTH C16, SOUTH C13

ADAM, CENTRAL FIGURE OF CLUSTERED MEDALLION C12 & C13 GLASS

"BOOKS, PICTURES, DESCRIPTIONS, STIR THE IMAGINATION CASTING THEIR SPELL; SEEING & EXPERIENCING THE REALITY IS TO POSSESS IT FOR EVER" Amon.

PÉRIGORD

APRIL 1956

we drove from CHARTRES
[intoxicatingly empty roads] through
'Impressionist' countryside to Leonardo's Tomb
& CHAUMONT; on thro' 'chateaux' country CHENONCEAUX to
NONTRON & charming BRANTÔME ON DRONNE, island & abbey town.

BRANTÔME, A TOWN WORTHY TO BE REFLECTED IN SO MANY WATERS.

LIKE SNAIL, WITH HOUSE ON BACK, WE TOOK OUR TENT WITH US, & "VOLCANO" HEATER FOR DAILY PICNICS.

'FAIRY' CASTLES WITH SPIKY SKYLINES TURRETS, TOWERS, BASTIONS CROWN THE HILLS

We wanted to see the haunts of Prehistoric Man along the Vézère, his caves, grottoes, shelters: LASCAUX, LA MOUTHE, FONT DE GAUME, LES COMBARELLES.

LES NOIX

A FRONT DOOR SOCIAL JOB WALNUT CRACKING. HATTED AGAINST THE SUN-TAP, TAP GO THE HAMMERS.

So we planned to visit the limestone countryside of the DORDOGNE, its cliffs, overhangs, ridges, gorges, causses, views & perched castles; its valleys & looping rivers which tumble in waterfalls & whirlpools singing over white pebbles; its Bastide towns, its villages, picturesque houses, historic churches, & its FOOD. All this astonishing, beautiful, hill country was a joyful empty playground for us, we walked, gambolled, revelled in it.

LES BLANCHISSEUSES STRAWHATTED, & RISING KNEELERS, SLOSH, SLAP, & RINSE, IN SPRING, POOL OR RIVER.

PIGEONNIERS OF EVERY STYLE, SPROUT FROM STEEP PITCHED ROOFS IN BEYNAC

BEYNAC, DOMME, SOUILLAC, ROCAMADOUR, SARLAT, CAHORS-SUR-LOT, ST CIRQUE LA POPIE, FIGEAC, CONQUES, ST CERE [LURÇAT], CARENNAC, MARTELL [LAVENDER] TURENNE, COLLONGES, BEAULIEU,—Towns each of distinctive character, each one of special interest to the visitor:

Blackthorn, cherry, apple, pear; peach, apricot orchards; blossom opening as we watched; walnut tree plantations, mulberries, vines, hillsides of lavender; daffodils, & many tiny flowers.

CARVED CAPITAL ABBEY CHURCH CONQUES HILLSIDE OF GORGE TERRACED TOWN

LARGE HEADS BIG HANDS

WE ATE GASTRONOMIC DELIGHTS:- FOIE GRAS, TRUFFLES, EPINARDS A LA CREME, CHAMPIGNONS, ENDIVE SALAD + HUILE DE NOIX, GATEAU, CROISSANTS, BRIOCHES, CAMEMBERT, ROQUEFORT CHEESE WE DRANK:- CIDRE BOUCHE, VIN DU PAYS, BLANQUETTE DE LIMOUX, & BEST OF ALL MONBAZILLAC.

SOUILLAC SCULPTURED COLUMN SACRIFICE OF ISAAC BY ABRAHAM. AMAZING.

OF ALL THIS MOST BOUNTIFUL FEAST OF SIGHTS, THE HIGHLIGHT FOR ME WAS THE VISIT TO LASCAUX.

ABOVE MONTIGNAC AMONG WALNUT & CHERRY TREES

On the cave paintings here we had set our sights. We approached the isolated hill top farm of M. & Mme. Baudry. Might we pitch our tent on their land for 3 nights?? & would they provide evening meals?

VINE COVERED TERRACE BY THE DORDOGNE

15 DAYS IN FRANCE; FERRY, PETROL, BEDS, MEALS, £23 EACH.

BEYNAC CASTLE PERCHED, AND TERRACE HOUSES CLINGING TO CLIFF FACE; BOATS AND TROUT FISHERS ON THE SHINING WATER, DORDOGNE.

'THIS ITINERARY WAS SO GOOD, THAT THE RECALLING & RECORDING OF IT HAVE STIMULATED ME TO COVER THESE EXACT TRACKS, VISITING THESE HAUNTS AT GREATER LEISURE.

We sat on their wistaria thatched terrace, where the land fell away
in steep grassy curves to give views across Montignac to the hills of
Guyenne, enjoying a meal composed entirely of their own
farm produce, & served by Madame who surely owned the
jolliest of all the sunny smiles in the region;-

their home pressed wine; stock pot soup; crusty rolls; endive;
their omelette aux truffes; cheeses; walnuts; crème de noix, café.

We pitched by cherries & vines on land which must be among the
oldest known to man, & slept, immediately above the powerful
cave paintings, so evocative, impressive, humbling.

PEACH

DANDELION
SALADE AT
BOURDEILLES &
BRANTOME

CHERRY

SCHOOL CHILDREN
IN SARLAT

I lay musing on these prehistoric artists, imagining how they
might collect & grind their earth pigments, bottling them
in marrow bones, mixing them on a scapula, applying
them with their fingers or with mosses or bristles etc.
Incredible animal magic, 30,000 B.C. ?

Then, back in April 1956, shortly after the cave's discovery,
Lascaux was quite uncommercialised, the entrance merely
a dip in the turfed ground, with just 4 seats round.

LAVANDE
DE
QUERCY

LAVENDER
distilled here
from local fields
almost spills
from the village
of MARTEL

NORMAN
GOTHIC
GABLED
COWLED

MORE
ROOF

PIGEONNIERS IN BEYNAC

MEDIEVAL HOUSES
OF
STREET CORNER
IN BEYNAC

CLOGS &

BESOM IN
COURTYARD OF
LION D'OR
HOTEL
MARTEL

We roamed the Vézère valley, haunts of prehistoric
man, to Les Eyzies with its cliff rock shelters,
caves, grottoes, & saw the engravings of La Mouthe
by paleolithic man 50000 BC, then the Font de Gaume
rhino, & Les Combarelles tiger & mammoth.

3 tiers
of tiled roof soffits

MUSINGS:-

"When I was at home, I was in a better place
but travellers must be content," said Touchstone.
                                              Shakespeare.

'Holidays, the only kind of cake
that makes bread eat better afterwards.'

'The best part of a holiday is the return from it,
the second best part is the planning & contemplation of it,
but the optimist looks forward with zest, finds
roses all the way & returns replenished.'

Francis Bacon, 1562-1626, said;-

'Travel in the younger sort is a part of education,
in the elder a part of experience.
Let diaries therefore be brought into use.'

'Tis man's worst deed
To let things that have been, run to waste
And in the unmeaning present sink the past.'

'Youth lives only in the years to come,
But Age, like double fronted Janus looks
All ways & ponders wisely on the past.'

A FIRST VISIT TO GREECE

[ATTICA & PELOPONNISOS]

Land of Myths & Legends;
of Homer's Iliad & Odyssey;
of the Delphic Oracle;
of Heroes; of Heracles;
of Marathon & Thermopylae;
of the Acropolis;
of Temples;
of Plato, Socrates, Pericles, Phidias;
of Sophocles, Euripides, Aristophanes, Aeschylus;
of Olympus, Parnassos, Pelion, Ossa, Taygetus;
of Spring Flowers & Paschal Candles.
Who would not wish to visit there?

EASTER · APRIL 1950

Καλο Πασχα

Extract from:
'WIND OF FREEDOM' 1943
Sir Compton Mackenzie [1883 – 1972]

" At 3.0 a.m. October 28 1940, Count Grazzi presented the Italian ultimatum to General Metaxas:-"And you will give my government the facilities it requests, and the free passage of troops to strategic points in Greece?" "No" said Metaxas.

The darkness & chill of that 3 oclock were symbolic of the dark & chill hour of human history in which the liberty of Europe seemed to be expiring.
Poland had been mangled, Finland overpowered, Norway overwhelmed, and Denmark had surrendered. Holland & Belgium had been trodden underfoot Hungary and Rumania lay prone, France had cried "Enough."

Yet Greece, disdaining the darkness & chill gave an answer which must outlive even the unimaginable touch of time. We who heard the news in Britain, we, fighting on in that dark hour alone, grasped the dear small hand of Greece offered to us in the darkness & found a new faith in the ultimate invincibility of free men."

NOWADAYS THE ANNUAL CELEBRATION OF 'OXI' DAY HAS COME TO SYMBOLISE THE SPIRIT OF THE NATION. OXI [ochi] = NO

ATHENS ΑΘΗΝΑΙ
EASTER STALLS, hung thickly with candles, lanterns, icons, line our main street.

Good Friday Candles

Easter Day Candles.

Ε. ΚΟΥΤΣΟΣ

SHAPELY PASCHAL LOAVES

SET WITH CRIMSON EGGS

LAMP & 3 ICONS SUSPENDED ABOVE BUS DRIVER'S SEAT

'You cannot imagine the altitude of our great pleasure
that you should come & trail your toes in Sparta.'

THUS WROTE EPHSTRATIOS SOUPOS, DIRECTOR OF STUDIES, HIGH SCHOOL, SPARTA,
IN A LETTER OF GRATITUDE FOR A CONSIGNMENT OF MATHEMATICAL INSTRUMENTS SENT BY STAFF & CHILDREN
OF WALTHAMSTOW HIGH SCHOOL TO THE PUPILS OF HIS WAR SCARRED & DEPRIVED GYMNASIUM, 1949

APRIL 1950 10.30 a.m.

From the billowing daffs of London, to Athens, a 2 day flight.
Refuel at Nice. [seaboard] Viking. 14 passengers, 2 abreast, 6 empty seats.
Chewing gum, sweets, earplugs on take-off, & personal care from most
attentive steward. Ham sandwiches brought to us two, we wrote & drew so
busily! "FOUNTAIN PENS LEAK AT HIGH ALTITUDES IN AN UNPRESSURISED PLANE" HE SAID,
& brought ammonia to rub away the offending blots on my coat. "I have
never seen anyone work so hard," said he. All the way the map below
was clearly visible & became an exciting reality. ROME 1920 HOTEL QUIRINALE 20.20

AN AMPLE TRAY SERVED
WITH GENEROUS MEALS
IN TEN DEPRESSED SLOTS

21.00 TABLE FOR 4.
JUST OUR PARTY ALONE.
TASTY FOOD, GOOD CUISINE.
LUXURIOUS SUITE ALL
INCLUSIVE IN FLIGHT TICKET.

A PACKED [LATE] EVENING IN ROME

20.30 PIAZZA OF ST PETER'S WITH
OBELISK, FOUNTAINS, FINE COLONNADE

PIAZZA DEL ESEDRA 24.00
WELCOME GOAL NEAR OUR HOTEL

23.00 COLOSSEUM FLOODLIT.
WE STOLE APPREHENSIVELY THRO'
THE DARK SPOOKY ARCHES INTO
THE HISTORIC ARENA,
BUT TOO NEAR MIDNIGHT
FOR TOTAL PLEASURE.

22.00 We bussed to the Vatican determined to seize this chance— & in moonlight—
walked its stately Forum, spacious, deserted, alone with our shadows, to St Peters, made
friends with the Papal black cat mewing for entrance. Then to the Colosseum, awesome
eerie, sinister in the shadows, & returning, stumbled unexpectedly
upon the Trajan Column, on our way thro' empty streets as midnight struck.

Amid
the babel
of foreign
tongues
we heard:-
"Are you the Professors from Britain?"
& a bridal bouquet of carnations was presented
TO EACH OF THE TWO OF US

Next day saw but 8 of us on the plane, bumping a
perilous shaky course between Greece's mountains
above the Corinth Canal, almost grazing its steep
sides, terrifying, to land thankfully in ATHENS,
spread wide below Hymettus; the Parthenon
just as one expects, gleaming above the city.

THIS WHOLE 2 DAY FLIGHT WE DEEMED QUITE EXCEPTIONAL VALUE FOR
MONEY, & WE SAVOURED IT MIGHTILY, EVERY PRECIOUS MINUTE OF IT.
WHAT A WELCOME AWAITED OUR ARRIVAL!

IN ATHENS, ΑΘΗΝΑΙ, & ATTICA

THE PARTHENON
ON THE ACROPOLIS ROCK OF ATHENS
SEEN FROM OUR TOILET WINDOW

Austere, yet bright little bedroom [no air conditioner, no T.V., Radio, phone] Work a day business men's hotel, [we the only women] cold water tap, tiny basin [with no stopper] marble floor, [no rugs] 2 hospital beds, [spotless white covers] all sweet & clean, 5/- per night, breakfast out. A petrol can eventually unearthed for our sumptuous carnation bouquets! Yet the flat roof gave views of Mt Parnis, Mt Pentelicon, & Mt Ymittos, & the toilet throne a regular & exclusive view of THE PARTHENON gleaming moonlit at night & floodlit over Easter!

Our 1st picnic was on the Acropolis. Fancy having it all to ourselves & finding a rough track of great granite boulders, like the last 200' to the top of Cairn Gorm, steep ways or easier ways freely alternative. Here on the renowned historic site at last! Look & ponder. The carved Greek characters on fallen marbles intrigued me [I was learning letter cutting.]

ASPHODEL AMONG THE FALLEN ACROPOLIS MARBLES

Easter time. Goods pack the shops, hang thickly from walls & ceilings, spill out on to pavements in an orgy of disarray. Piles of oranges bar the way, taxis hoot, tram bells clang, cocks crow from roofs in the thronging streets. Our quarter is as crowded as approaches to Murrayfield on International Day.

BOOT BLACKS IN STREETS, IN SQUARES, AT CORNERS, IN SHOPS

THE SHOE CLEANING TRADE SEEMS TO THRIVE.

FOOT STOOL EQUIPMENT BOX, SURELY AN A HEIR LOOM.

On violet crowned Hymettus, bees swarmed above sheets of vetch giving us a honey breakfast each morning. We sampled marble on Pentelicon, & ferreted out a Laurion bus for a 6 ml walk to Cape Sunion. There stood the Temple of Poseidon, grand in its isolation, the cliff, the marble columns deserted.

TEMPLE OF POSEIDON [WELL NAMED] ON CAPE SUNION OF ATTICA

SURELY A WELCOME SIGHT TO MARINERS RETURNING TO ATHENS.

No fence, no gate, no by your leave. Just wander where you will among the pillars of this flowery headland while characters from archaic myths & legends crowd the mind.

A lightning dip in a sandy cove (just as we do in the W. Highlands) our 1st bath, for Athens suffers severe water shortage, then bus back through villages gay with flags & bunting. Every other man carried a Paschal lamb alive or dead, loaves nesting red dyed eggs, & purple stocks.

You've heard of course, of the magical clear atmosphere in Greece. We hope yet to see it. And today, anything more like Edinburgh in Feb, I can't imagine. I'm dad as for Ben Nevis! Yesterday's sea bath dip may be our last in spite of tempting seas.

GOOD FRIDAY EVENING. ATHENS.

Ecclesiastics made a colourful note in Good Friday Procession. As it approached with funereal music, spectators, lining the streets [& carrying purple stocks, a sign of grief] lit their flickering candles, window candles glittered, & the bier procession passed slowly between twinkling rivers of light.

EASTER SATURDAY EVENING

By evening, all stalls away, streets neat, & now cheery with strings of lights, bunting, flags. Restaurants closed. we starved! Parthenon floodlit.

At midnight, every white candle is lit. From our roof we watched the serpent of light descend the zig zag path of LYCABETTUS, that rock, which rises dramatically from the centre of Athens, like N. Berwick Law.

CACTI ON THE WINDING TRACK DOWN THE CONE OF LYCABETTUS

TRAVEL 1950

What problems beset travellers on long distance buses! The various obscure depots all at sixes & sevens; confused & dislocated by ravages of war & not yet reorganised.

NO BUS TIME TABLES! "Go here." "Go there". Endless conflicting instructions.

What precious hours we used, tracking down a Sparta bus! REAL SPADE WORK!

THE MOUNTAIN ROAD, ARGOS TRIPOLIS TO SPARTA

Now FOR SPARTA [PELOPONISSOS an Open Air Museum & Rock Garden proliferating flowers.]

5.0 a.m Rise. Walk the 1¼ mls to specified bus depot for 7.0 bus

8.30 Still waiting, depressed & irritated by noise & argument.

9.00 We are hurried on to bus full of University Professors, off to SPARTA for a first celebration since the war. The Byzantine Union of Archaeologists.

STONE TOTEMS TOPPED THE WALLS

Scironian Cliffs. Saronic Gulf. Scenery, quite W. Highland, we felt at home! Islands, halcyon seas.

CORINTH CANAL, road block, all identities inspected. Fire arms? Civil war— had till recently closed the Peninsula. [whole battle fleets were rolled across this ISTHMUS in ancient times] Heracles country, Argive Plain, then up over 4,000' to Tripolis. Then miles of potholed road, the bus lolloping, flinging itself about, a hellish crawl for 3+ hours, we twice broke down! Then the fair Eurotas Valley backed by snowy TAYGETOS RANGES, & so to SPARTA 6.0 city of Leonidas.

WE RECALLED:- "VICTORIOUS WITH, OR DEAD ON YOUR SHIELD". WHAT SHOULD WE FIND?

Communist Guerillas — FROM PAINTED VASE (6 BC)

HERACLES WEARING LION'S SKIN, [KNOTTED PAWS LION'S HEAD MASK] WITH HIS PATRONESS THE SEATED ATHENE

6.0 pm

Ephstratios Soupos & retinue of scholastics to meet & escort us. 7.0 pm, Official Reception mounted for Byzantine Union. We are invited & deemed honoured guests, presented to the Bishop, Mayor, Prefect, & escorted to centre front seats. Several speeches delivered, then Easter Rolls & Paschal Eggs [purple] ceremoniously cracked against one's neighbour's. An unbroken egg from this contest means 12 happy months. After Greek National Anthem & much chat [French, German, older generation rarely speaks English,] we withdrew, escaping hungrily to seek our 1st good meal of this long & eventful day, & to muse upon Lycourgos, Menelaus, etc.

WARRIOR, MARBLE, EXCAVATED SPARTA 1925

Is it King Leonidas of Sparta, killed in helmet holding the Pass of Thermopylae against Persians of Xerxes 480 BC?

IN & AROUND SPARTA LACONIA APRIL 1950

Next morning we quite unexpectedly found ourselves to be the centre of an impressive
Official Welcome by the Mayor, Corporation, Staff & VIth Forms of the Gymnasium & again
ushered to centre front seats. Many orations delivered, [in which we were "honoured" "noble" guests,
one was in verse by a VI th form boy] extolling Greek heroism &
the stand for freedom made by Britain. All was very
solemn & Greek to us. THEN CAME THE SHOCK :- we were,
without warning, ushered to the platform & pressed to
reply. To our increasing delight & ease, gales of laughter
greeted our extemporised words [translated phrase by phrase] which
mainly centred on the Plane Tree from Thermopylae [now thriving in the Walthamstow garden,]
& the common use of Mathematical symbols, [MENTION OF THE ELGIN MARBLES WAS AVOIDED!] Then hounded
by the press, we nearly missed the chocolate/fruit delicacies which accompanied curacoa.

NEAR SPARTA — EUROTAS shallows & olive groves compete for our picnics. Peasants launder in the deep swirls.

Now, our jaunts into Sparta are enlivened by handshakes & little assorted presents from friends.

From such acclaim, we sought refuge in the countryside, enjoying the
olive groves, mulberry & plane trees in young leaf, & wandering the Eurotas
shingly islands & silvery shallows between white poplars, oleanders, aloes,
sallows, cypresses, & brilliant green of reeds. We thought of shepherds'
pipes. Would Pan appear? Would we panic? Nymphs there might
well be. Frogs in chorus reminded us of Aristophanes [very voluble,
insistant, & not at all in laconic style!] & a friendly tortoise shared our picnic.

CHURCH OF PANTANASSA MISTRA
Seen from the ruined gate of Monemvasie.

Lizards basked & sported around rock crevices

What a snowy wall rose behind Sparta! Bandits still lurked in
the hills, we heard. Rebels were fighting here a few months ago.
Bullet holes freckled the school walls. Our kind attentive hosts
wished to drive us about, but there is only one car in Laconia, the Prefect's. 2 TAXIS!

MISTRA VILLAGE has its large central Plane Tree. A prize Tree stock threw a purple cascade from an upstairs window.

We retreated to Mistra, a one time walled cultural centre of
the Byzantine Empire built on a spur of Taygetos, commanding
views over the rich Eurotas plain lying between 2 mountain walls,
& now a mere shell of a city.
We climbed the steep hillside jewelled with rioting flowers
to pantiled vaulted churches beautifully frescoed, up &
up past palace walls to the castle view above this ruinous city.

Back in the village, locals who gathered round, gave us an impromptu concert, clarinet & dulcimer,
till the little country bus came. Timeless, these friendly pleasure loving Greeks.

Returning to Athens, we & the coach, again suffered 63 kms of potholed road to Tripolis, then 260 kms
to Athens at a terrifying breakneck speed, hair pin bends & cliff drops notwithstanding.

There Elena Papazoglu met us, & later came to visit our Athens of the North & W. Highland panoramas.

PELOPONNISOS. Argolis & Corinth, Arcadia, Laconia, Messinia, Achaia & Elis.

Extraordinary & astonishing that these sites of antiquity, with their upright or fallen stones should lie open & unfenced, approached only by faintly worn tracks in the year 1950. Remote & wild, the very air is numinous. Alone, & invaded by a haunting mystery, one is lost in the echoes & eras of measureless time. Flowers exceed all expectations.

The powerfully sculptured BULL, One of the most impressive of exhibits in the OLYMPIA MUSEUM

THE HERMES OF PRAXITELES, not yet released from wartime hibernation

Here, the imposing gate of 'golden' MYCENAE, fiercely dramatic. Tombs, walls, all monumental, potent, terrific. Would Agamemnon's ghost appear, or Clytemnestra weave a spell?

LISTEN! Here, down in the domed earthbound stone Treasury, a curious vibrating note of sound. What is it? LOOK UP! Hundreds of circling bees!!!

The savage Cyclopean walls of TIRYNS over awed us. [HERACLES]

IN LAVISH PROFUSION, APRIL
AN ECSTASY OF FLOWERS

EPIDAURUS enchanted. (Asklepios) Complete solitude. Alone in the great open air theatre, seating 14,000, we in turn dropped a pebble, & declaimed from the arena, to be heard with ringing clarity in "the gods". ACOUSTIC PERFECTION!

wearing lion mask & using knob kerry club
FROM (&) AMPHORA
HERACLES WRESTING TRIPOD FROM APOLLO. THE PELOPONNESUS IS HERACLES COUNTRY.

NAUPLIA with its castle crowned Acropolis, & campanula cascading from seagirt rocks, charmed. We bathed, dawdled climbed & gazed.

BASSAE set high in stark mountain country, isolated & remote & well preserved. What a heightened contrast to find the site of OLYMPIA so romantic & pastoral. Fat sheep graze under olives by the silvery winding Alpheus.

OF HOMER'S ILIAD
ACHILLES, HELMET RAISED, & AJAX, REST SPEARS FOR A GAME. FROM FIGURED AMPHORA VASE (6BC

NEMEA: Away in the Argive Plain HERACLES COUNTRY the Temple Remains looked forgotten in the pastoral setting. Would the Nemean lion appear? No!

HERACLES!
ANOTHER FRIENDLY TORTOISE

ANCIENT upper CORINTH: As we stood among the remaining seven monolithic pillars looking across the Gulf, PERACHORA called; so we later drove that wild & beautiful country to the renowned site so blissfully & astonishingly situated. What a pearl it is!

THE HEAD PERSEUS
A HIP BAG WILL CARRY
IN EAGER PURSUIT OF GORGON'S HEAD
FROM FIGURED CUP (6BC

Athenian Black/Red Figure Vases fascinate once the eye is turned on the curved surfaces have remarkable delicacy of line (6BC

The austere beauty of this Pelops peninsula, specially appealing to W. Highland lovers, the seagirt flower jewelled earth, the very spirit of the place, brought a host of names leaping to the mind:- Aeschylus, Aristophanes, Asklepios, Homer, Odysseus, Menelaus & so on.

PELOPONNESUS, RAIL & ROAD. 1951

SARONIC GULF, & CLIFFS FROM WHICH THE ROBBER SCIRON HURLED TRAVELLERS

UNTIL THESEUS FINALLY INFLICTED ON HIM THE SAME FATE.

A train journey round this Peninsula is an adventure in itself, incidents & sights to R & Left above & below, & within the carriage. But, today in 1951, the Athens ticket office is ¼ hour from the station; 30 m.p.h. is barely the average speed, long waits for trains [always late] & longer waits for connections, therefore time to make friends & even to visit their homes for sustenance!

At stations boys besieged the passengers with livers impaled on sticks, girls offered ropes of rosy apples. When I wanted to sketch [Alpheus] the train was held by a friendly guard. Coffins were offloaded at rural stations & left lying, 2 of them.
SOME TRAINS, WE HEARD, ARE SO CROWDED, FOLK RIDE ON STEPS, ROOF & FOOTBOARDS.

LANDSCAPE PATTERNS

THE MARCH-APRIL CURRANT VINES OF CORINTH PLAIN

sharing a bit of basic common knowledge in an Algebra Book

sharing local produce, a slice of lemon.

Barefoot peasants with apples for sale

A diversion for schoolboys

Megaspelion Gorge

In our homely companionable coach we met by chance the Region Prefect, Ilis, just returned from Edinburgh! "C'est une verité— L'Athenes du Nord avec son Acropole" he agreed; also Cassandra, who lit the 1949 Olympic Flame; Daphne & Iris, who shared with P. the mysteries of πR^2 & $L^2 - \beta^{\frac{3}{2}}$; peasants, who laughed & conversed happily in sign language; school boys, who giggled & nudged as I drew; & best of all a helpful Discus Thrower, who knew the Langada Pass to be now open, & would himself be crossing it tomorrow, so our apprehensions were over. NOT A SINGLE ATHENS AUTHORITY WAS ABLE TO PROVIDE INFORMATION RE THE PASS!

We gasped at the beauty of almond orchards in perfection of blossom; fig trees in young leaf, like candelabras; hedges of madonna lilies; lemon orchards fruit laden; fields of asphodels waving like a ballet of pearls; snowy mountain peaks above, blue seas below.
A MOST EXCITING LEISURELY CRAWL VIA CORINTH, PYRGOS, OLYMPIA, TO KALAMATA.

A FRACTION OF THE REMOTE & DESOLATE PASS THRO' TAYGETOS TO SPARTA 38 mls 6,000 ft 3½ hrs

5 of us in an old Humber survived crossing the formidable Langada Pass of TAYGETOS among rugged wild soaring peaks & plunging gorges, across questionable bridges & chasms on this narrow precipitous mule-jeep road, pot holed & gashed by ice, snow, rock falls, with fir forests of jackals polecats vultures, wolves! 3½ GRIM, BREATHTAKING PANIC RIDDEN HOURS!
KALAMATA TO SPARTA, A THRILLING RIDE

APPROACHING ATHENS LATER, THE SKYLINE WITH LYCABETTUS WAS A SMALL VERSION OF CUILLIN! MIMOSA WAS CASCADING GOLD, & ORANGE BLOSSOM SPREAD A FRAGRANCE THRO' THE CITY. *Thinking of the Philosophers, Statesmen, Dramatists, Sculptors of the Golden Age, Greeks renowned for their enterprise & wisdom, how very odd these friendly helpful locals, cannot read a map!*

SOME ISLANDS OF THE SARONIC GULF 1950

ΑΙΓΙΝΑ

SPONGES SLUNG BETWEEN TREES

MENDING NETS

Lord Byron writes of "The Isles of Greece / Where burning Sappho loved & sung"

DECOR OF BLACK FIGURE WATER JAR (6 BC)

ΣΑΠΦΟ

SAPPHO (HYDRIA, KALPIS SHAPE VASE)

"We must set foot on AEGINA"

Up at 6.30. Underground to Piraeus, on to unlabelled boat [hopefully not setting out for America!] Salamis, Saronic Gulf, Doric Sea, W Highland scenery, & chilly breezes all the way across to the island. A ramshackle old Ford bumped us the rough road up to the TEMPLE of APHAIA, locals on the way joined for a lift sitting on the bonnet! Look! the Temple, in superb setting, panoramic island views, & each rock cranny spectacular with flowers.

BEE ORCHIS, a thrilling find in the rioting profusion of wild flowers.

In the only hotel (seedy, & down at heel,) we occupied the best centre front balconied room. Bare boards, electric light, but no running water! Another swim required! Dictionary mislaid, so to get a boiled egg, a hen & egg had to be drawn, & a pan of steaming hot water. Restaurant full of men, all black coated, fingering alabaster comfort beads. WHERE WERE THE WOMEN? We knew the answer. Heavy rain, wind, & thunder storms overnight.

"POROS next," we said, breakfasting on our balcony, & looking down on to the jetty. 9.30. On to a boat, the only foreigners among a jostle of locals, livestock & coffins; planes skimming overhead & goats disembarking.

Off the island of Methana a priest from a coracle joins us to the island of Poros.

The cone of POROS rises dazzling white from blue seas. Much chat here with French speaking Greek who knew Scotland.

Here everything is enchanting & little gifts rain upon us:- small bouquets of stocks thrown down to us from an upstairs window box, hot prawns on forks presented by little 'Marathon' runners as we sat at our picnic on the hill top, pistachio nuts from a shepherd in fustanella, & posies from jolly sure footed boys who leaped among rocks & bushes on the steep hillside.

FRESHLY COOKED PRAWNS SENT ACROSS

One could almost toss a coin into the lemon groves of Argolis across the strait.

A cherry brandy on the sparkling water front; katsoules at sunset: a hotel, classic without shabby within; then goodbye to this delectable island. Approach now the formidable stark unpromising rocky cliffs of Hydra. Yet round the

AGILE BOYS LEAP AS TO THE MANNER BORN

PEASANT

POROS

IN FUSTANELLA

headland nestles a narrow cosy bay, colourful boats & steep amphitheatre of handsome white houses, steep white alleyways, step ladders to me. Tombazi Sch of Fine Arts up to high monastery, climbed, & explored; flowers & views marvelled upon. Our return boat anchored by the island of MONI, giving us a swim in translucent jade waters.

MILOS, DELOS, ANDROS, MYKONOS, of the CYCLADES; PATMOS, KOS, ETC of the DODECANESE; SPORADES....'ISLANDS', THE WORD ITSELF CASTS A SPELL.

18

"Life piled on life Were all too little..."
said Ulysses. [Lord Tennyson]

ZEUS COUNTRY. The mountain spine backdrops, contemplated with awe. Mt Dictus Cave, the snows of Mt Ida, & Mt Juktas; Zeus buried here.

A VISIT TO CRETE 1951

Goodbye
to Cape Sunion,
Aegina, Poros, Hydra.
Our little plane, almost
skimming the water, winged its
way above the CYCLADES, [their long
peninsulas, rank upon rank,] above
Canea & the rocky profile of "Cretan Zeus"
named Mount Juktas; to land us after 1 hour,
in HERAKLION

Again here we found such friendly folk. The
Hotelier attentive & kindness itself. Kyria
Sylligardos loaded us with superb posters.
Bank clerks & school boys, full of eager curiosity,
were keen to try their English on us. Ody & Dio
Apostolacos, Chrys & Ares Koutsi, befriended us.

Now for chalky hill track walks, & sunny
picnics among olives, figs, & carpets of irises, &
of course, Sir Arthur Evans' excavated
Palace of KNOSSOS revealing the
high levels of Early Minoan
Civilisation and fine
works of Art.

FRESCO FRAGMENT CALLED 'LA PARISIENNE' (17 BC?)
IS SHE PASSING A LOVING CUP? THE BUNCHED SCARF BEHIND HER HEAD IS A SACRAL KNOT

STANDING FIGURE OF SNAKE GODDESS OR PRIESTESS. [FIGURINE STATUETTE IN FAIENCE]
Fitting jacket, bare breasts, laced waist, tiered skirt.

THESEUS BATTLES with the MINOTAUR

"THE BLUE BIRD" WALL PAINTING FROM THE HOUSE OF FRESCOES, KNOSSOS C17 BC

THE NOBLE THE PRIEST KING PAINTED RELIEF PALACE, KNOSSOS
LARGER THAN LIFE

2" FIGURES OF FRESCO FRAGMENT RITUAL DANCE IN SACRED GROVE (18 BC?) KNOSSOS

Companions on our CAPTAIN
MINOAN JUG OCTOPUS ORNAMENT
BULL LEAPING FRESCO
DOUBLE AXE DECOR
Leisurely return sail

All the spoils of Crete remain here in Heraklion Mus. How we gloated over the exhibits!
Come in the Spring to enjoy countryside, flowers, Gulf of Mirabello, Mallia, Gournia,
Palaikastro, Zacro, Tylissos, Phaistos, & so on.

BIRDS, WASPS, FROGS, OF ARISTOPHANES, & MULTITUDES OF WILD FLOWERS IN SPRINGTIME GREECE.

HERACLES & BIRDS

STYMPHALIAN BIRDS

DECOR ON CUP & COBC

GODDESS ATHENE INTRODUCES HER PROTÉGÉ HERACLES TO OLYMPIAN DEITY ZEUS

THE ZEALOUS HERACLES, WITH CLUB, WEARS THE LION'S SKIN, HEAD MASK FLUNG BACK.

EUPHORBIA

GERANIUM

LATHYRUS

ADRIATIC

ALBANIA

YUGOSLAVIA

MACEDONIA

THRACE

TURKEY

SEA OF MARMARA

THESSALONIKA

EPIRUS

OLYMPUS

METEORA PENEUS

OSSA

HELLESPONT

CARDANELLES

TROY

T U R K E Y

PINDUS MT

THESSALY

VOLOS

SPORADES

LESBOS

DAPHNE

IONIAN SEA

LAMIA

THERMOPYLAE

EUBOEA

A E G E A N

GLADIOLUS

GIONA

PARNASSUS

ITHAKA MISOLONGHI

DELPHI

PATRAS

MARATHON

ATHENS PIRAEUS

CORINTH

ERYMANTHUS

NEMEA

MYCENAE

ELEUSIS EPIDAURUS

CYCLADES

SEA

MEDITERRANEAN

PELOPONNESUS

OLYMPIA

PYRGOS

BASSAE

TRIPOLIS

ARGOS

NAUPLIA

ARGOLIS

DODECANESE

IBERIS

SPARTA TAYGETUS

DAPHNE DIANTHUS

MULLEIN

ALTHAEA

HOLLYHOCK

ITHAEA

"As the stars in the sky, so the sporadic scattering of islands in the seas of Greece."

IPOMOEA

CRETE

GREECE

PRACLION KNOSSOS

IDA

GORTYN DICTE CORINTH

ZAKRO

COUNTRY OF THE ILIAD & ODYSSEY

PHAISTOS

SEA

ANEMONE

Said Ulysses:– "I will drink
Life to the lees–—

"Yet all experience is an arch where thro'
Gleams the untravelled world whose margins fade
Forever & for ever when I move." Alfred Lord Tennyson.

CYCLAMEN

"SKETCHING BELT." 3 bottles Indian Ink in 3 densities, superseded in later years by ball points & felt pens.

GREECE. A POST SCRIPT 1951 & '63

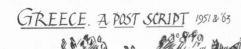

A KNOCKOUT SPECTACLE,
THIS CARAVAN IN THE EMPTY PLAIN!
YOUNG WOMEN'S SKIRTS WERE STIFF WITH PETTICOATS. [BARE FEET]

On subsequent visits to Greece we made our way N·of Athens & my travel diaries are specially lyrical on the following:-

Peasants in covered wagons or open carts on the Thessalian Plain, going off to market & pausing while the women water their pitchers from a wayside raised well;

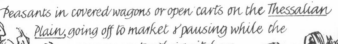

Mountain village Squares, each with gushing fountain under a shady plane tree, as at Macrynitsa on Pelion, with Ossa & Olympus beyond, & the Garden of the Hesperides below;

LOADED MULES CLIMB THE STEEP TRACK AT MACRYNITSA

Boy shepherds piping, & peasant women spinning from rollocks of wool.

Storks, wading & nest building on the Plain of the Peneus;

SPINNING

Rhamnos, N·of Marathon, a remote unspoilt site of antiquity above blue seas, scarlet anemones rioting;

The friendly tortoise among bee orchis; stocks, & wavy pink anemones blowing on the hill of Thermopylae;

RHAMNOS

Delphi on Parnassus, dramatic beyond words; 1951

Details in my sketch pad of delightful visits here, await future recording.

& the breathtaking Meteora; rock towers rising like black dolomites from the flat plain. We sat by a stream listening to nightingales

The brief notes on this page give only the merest flavours & reminders of full & vivid days

EACH VISIT TO ATHENS GAVE FURTHER CONTACT WITH KYRIA SOUPOS, & ELENA PAPAZOGLU WHO LATER VISITED EDINBURGH

EDINBURGH TO LONDON

BY MAIN LINE RAIL
BREAKING JOURNEYS OCCASIONALLY
TO CALL AT :-

BERWICK ON TWEED

NEWCASTLE ON TYNE

DURHAM

YORK

PETERBOROUGH

also mentioning FOUR
Cathedrals away to the east of this line,
for which one would change trains :-

BEVERLEY, LINCOLN, NORWICH, ELY.

MUCH TO SEE IN THE CITY OF EDINBURGH

in the Old Town,
the New Town,
the Villages,
& environs;

the Art Galleries,
the Museums,
Sports Centres,
Zoo, etc...

ST·GILES'
CATHEDRAL
CROWN TOWER

K·CHARLES II

HEART OF
MIDLOTHIAN

JOHN KNOX

The more you look
The more you see,

The more you see
The more you muse.

ROOF, GREAT HALL OF PARLIAMENT HOUSE

THE PALACE OF HOLYROOD HOUSE

After Elena Papazoglu had mused in the 6 museums, & keenly
enthused about many other sights of the Old Town between
Castle & Palace, I asked what she had enjoyed most of all.
"The Cairn of Arthur's Seat!" said with unreserved exuberance.

FOR DRAWINGS & NOTES ABOUT EDINBURGH
IN EXCESS OF THESE THREE PAGES, SEE:-
"PEN PORTRAITS OF EDINBURGH" ALSO BY D.A.GOODCHILD

EDINBURGH, CITY OF HILLS, VIEWPOINTS, VISTAS.

The city Palace of Holyrood House with hills & sheep almost on its portal, has 2 leg stretching climbs at hand:- CALTON HILL to the N; ARTHUR'S SEAT to the S; with CASTLE HILL to the W. up the ROYAL MILE. What a unique & enviable situation! This view, my favourite, from the low ground level of Queen's Park, in its way, competes with those from hill tops. A dancing skyline.

FROM PRINCES ST RAISE YOUR EYES & LOOK E BEYOND SCOTT MONUMENT TO CALTON HILL. & SEE :- NELSON MON· NATIONAL MON· D·STEWART MON· & CITY OBSERVATORY. AT HAND ARE:- REGISTER HOUSE, WELLINGTON STATUE, POST OFFICE & N·B·CLOCK TOWER.

MAGICAL VIEW

FROM ST ANDREW SQ. LOOK ACROSS THE FIRTH TO THE HILLS OF FIFE.

THESE VIEWS NEVER FAIL TO GRATIFY AS DO MANY OTHERS

VIEWS FROM CASTLE ROCK ARE STUPENDOUS

PART OF LONG SKYLINE FROM PRINCES ST ACROSS GARDENS TO TO CASTLE CRAG

No shopping areas, however attractive, stand a chance with Eléna Papazoglu if there is a hill to be climbed with such views from the summit. "I'm much happier grappling with a hill than a shopping list" she said, setting foot on Arthur's Seat. Back in Princes St her adjective was "stunning" for the changing view all along from E to W.

VIEW OF CASTLE ROCK, FROM W·END PRINCES ST WITH 2 CHURCHES ST JOHNS & ST CUTHBERT'S. IN SILHOUETTE AGAINST THE SUN

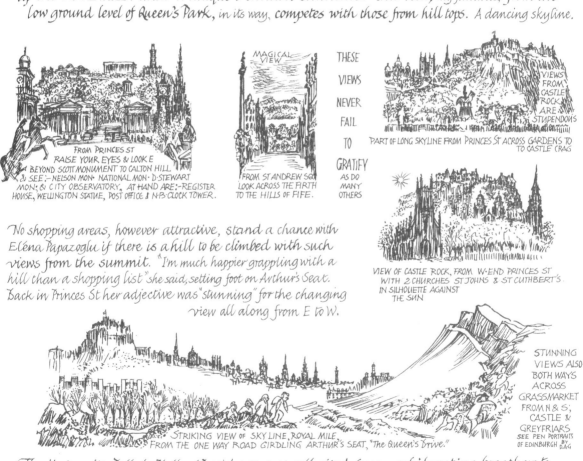

STRIKING VIEW OF SKY LINE, ROYAL MILE, FROM THE ONE WAY ROAD GIRDLING ARTHUR'S SEAT, "The Queen's Drive."

STUNNING VIEWS ALSO BOTH WAYS ACROSS GRASSMARKET FROM N & S; CASTLE & GREYFRIARS SEE PEN PORTRAITS OF EDINBURGH BY D.A.G

The University Pollock Halls of Residence are well sited for an exhilarating breather to be enjoyed from their very doorstep. In seconds a student can be up on the Radical road under Salisbury Crags, in minutes on the summit of Arthur's Seat, in minutes more plunging in the Commonwealth Pool

ARTHUR'S SEAT & SALISBURY CRAGS

Arthur's Seat takes on a different profile from every point of view. This one, to my mind most clearly delineates the noble lion profile. Climb this city mountain each day for a month, *attacking from various points* & your legs will be in form for Everest! Lucky Edin. folk! So many hills at hand!

CALTON HILL

FLAT TOPPED & SEEN HERE FROM PICARDY PLACE, ELM ROW, BLENHEIM PLACE. "SAID R.L.S." OF ALL PLACES FOR A VIEW, CALTON HILL IS PERHAPS THE BEST. SAID YLÉNA PAPAZOGLOU, "SO THIS IS YOUR ACROPOLIS OF THE NORTH WITH ITS PARTHENON! HUMPH! LET'S GO UP!"

HERE, A ROW OF SINGLE STOREY VILLAS [PLAYFAIR 1830] AS SEEN FROM THE FRONT, BUT LOOK BEHIND!

VIEW S. DOWN ST DAVID STREET TO THE BLACK NEEDLE OF SCOTT MONUMENT, ALWAYS ENCOUNTERED BY ME WITH FRESH ASTONISHMENT. MANY OTHER SINGULAR VISTAS AROUND

Playground on high; bird sanctuary below.

DUDDINGSTON LOCH.

The high level 3+mls of Queen's Drive round A. Seat, passes two lochs. This one, below, the 3rd, is never without its complement of duck & geese for children to feed

613' NORTH BERWICK LAW

Another peak to climb; the astonishing volcanic cone jutting up behind North Berwick. Yléna said, "So you have also a Lycabettus, let's reach those whalebones."

FROM ALL THE MANY HILL VIEWPOINTS BETWEEN CALTON HILL & THE PENTLANDS, THE RAILWAY & ROAD BRIDGES OVER THE RIVER FORTH ARE VISIBLE. [SEE "HILLS OF EDINBURGH" by D.A.G.]

THE BASS ROCK

a "sugar loaf" rising sheer from the sea; amazing spectacle seen from land or sea. Gannets galore! [see "EAST LOTHIAN" also by D.A.G.]

When your train has left the city behind, you may catch a glimpse of these 2 latter outcrops if you look N. to the Firth of Forth. What geological prizes Edinburgh has!

BERWICK ON TWEED

FROM THE TRAIN SEE:- DUNBAR P. CHURCH, BARNS NESS LIGHT HSE, TORNESS NUCLEAR POWER STN, AYTON CASTLE.

These 4 seaward landmarks, the rounded braes of the petering Lammermuirs [brilliantly gilded in June; whin; gorse;] then more coastal views, bring us to BERWICK ON TWEED; the pearl in my oyster, for I had never suspected what delights this compact small town can give. One can girdle it in an hour's easy scenic walking - 'treading on air':—

Bright November morn, 800 FROST From Railway Station down wooded hillside, past lily pond, to the waters of the dear old Tweed, & Norman Castle wall remnants.

Look up! Mighty arches of curving Rly Viaduct.

Swans, gulls, bridges, Quay walls, C18 houses, Custom House, steps up, steps down, salmon cobles, seals.

Pier 1810-21 £61,000, Gracious houses, Fortifications [evidence; a violent past] Elizabethan ramparts, Cumberland bastion, Megs Mount etc, idyllic turfed walks [high level & low,] Golf, & beaches.

ROYAL BORDER BRIDGE 1850 NOBLE SIGHT 28 ARCHES

NARROW & DEEP GUILDHALL C18 WITH CURFEW BELL CLOCK TOWER, BUTTER MARKET BELOW & BEHIND. APPROACH UP 16 STEPS CHARTER STREET MARKET WEDS, SATS.

COWPORT TO RAMPARTS & BARRACKS

RLY STN IT STILL WORKS DRINKING FOUNTAIN

MARYGATE leading N. STEPS TO RAMPARTS

LOW TIDE - RIVER TWEED, & A TUMBLE OF CASTLE ROCK RUINS.

BERWICK BRIDGE C17 15 ARCHES & RECESSES

ROYAL TWEED BRIDGE 1928

Now, after this sea girt walk:- Marygate; Art Gallery & Museum; Market; Guildhall; vaulted Butter Market for coffee; Wine & Spirit Museum closed; & so on. A spell of days must be dated to absorb these, & other delights, at leisure. Train for Newcastle now due.

WATCH FOR LINDISFARNE, HOLY ISLAND CHARMING ALNMOUTH & ITS YACHTS, & 13 SHINING PENNANTS ST. NICHOLAS CATHEDRAL, NEWCASTLE ON TYNE

IN NEWCASTLE UPON TYNE

SEEKING OUT & SKETCHING SOME OF THE
INTERESTING FEATURES SEEN
BETWEEN THE UNIVERSITY
AND THE RIVER
23·12·83

FLIGHT OF SCULPTURED SWANS ABOVE POOL CIVIC CENTRE

LOOK UP TO 4 GOLD CORNER FIGURES

13 GLEAMING PENNANTS

CROWN-LANTERN TOWER St NICHOLAS CATHEDRAL

VESTIBULE LAING ART GALLERY

BLACK GATE IN WALL 1247 HOUSE ABOVE 1618 HOLDS AN EXHIBITION OF BAGPIPES

6 LIGHT ROYAL ARCADE

KEEP 1177. GREAT HALL WELL NORMAN CHAPEL (a gem) Oh! the climb!

So much is striking:-
the lantern crown tower of
St. Nicholas Cathedral;
the spire of All Saints Church
on its commanding site;
the Tyne Bridge
& 5 others of various design;
the curved frontages in The Side;
the timber houses of Sandhill;
&, OF COURSE, GREY St.

I enjoyed ferreting out the C13
Blackfriars {COFFEE HSE INFORMATION CRAFTS ETC} & Wall remains;
a picnic between showers under the
Durham Tower; found the Old Assembly
Ballroom 1779, & the many Museums,
Theatres, & shall always remember
the C15 Font Canopy of St. Andrew's Ch.

ALL ENJOYED, DEC 22, 23, WHILE OTHERS WERE SHOPPING.

1st FLOOR OF 5 STOREY TIMBER HOUSE C16-C17 IN SANDHILL

BESSIE SURTEES ELOPED FROM THIS WINDOW WITH LORD ELDON 1772, WHO LATER BECAME LORD CHANCELLOR

HANDSOME SPIRE OF ALL SAINTS ROUND CHURCH PERCHED ABOVE TYNE

4+2 LAMPS PORTICO THEATRE ROYAL 1837, GREY St.

J.G. JOICEY MUSEUM

TAM O SHANTER CARVINGS, BEWICK, ETC· A UNIQUE MUSEUM

DOME OF GUILDHALL GEORGIAN, CURVED COLONNADED FRONT.

HANCOCK MUSEUM BRASS NATURAL HIST· OCEANIC ART

HATTON GALLERY UNIVERSITY, TEMP. CLOSED.

ANTIQUITIES MUSEUM ROMAN ETC [UNIVERSITY]

HOW TO PROP BROLLY & DRAW IN RAIN??

DOME OF KEELMAN'S HOSPITAL 1701 KEEL BOATS CARRIED COAL.

QUAYSIDE 1 4 7 2 JOHN WESLEY GRANITE COLUMN

TYNE BRIDGE 1928

HIGH LEVEL BGE. RAIL, ROAD, FOOTWAY 1849

SWING BRIDGE

MY 2 DAY VISIT WAS DOGGED WITH RAIN & SODDEN SKETCH PAGES

3 OF NEWCASTLE'S 6 TYNE BRIDGES. LIFTS TO QUAYSIDE IN PYLONS OF SINGLE SPAN BRIDGE

IN COURTYARD OF TRINITY HOUSE, BROAD CHARE.

THE CITY OF DURHAM
A FEW HOURS ROAMING ON A LATE NOVEMBER DAY '83

CATHEDRAL & CASTLE AS FROM N.

SANCTUARY KNOCKER N. DOOR

Seen from the railway, how magnificently this great Norman Cathedral presides upon its rock, towering up & dominating the city at its feet. An impelling sight which never fails to astonish, so be ready to look E· before you enter the station.

TOWERS OF DURHAM CATHEDRAL, rising from above the trees, fortress like in its massive grandeur.

E END SCRIBE (VAULT)

TWIN CORBELS (NAVE)

N·W·WALL

[TODAY'S PICNIC, S·FACING NOOK BENEFICENT WARM SUN]

THE DUN COW N·W·WALL

CATHEDRAL SEEN FROM S.

3 ARCHED PREBEND BRIDGE

Here we idled in low go-car

The River Wear, like a steep sided moat looping round 3½ sides of the rock, is crossed by 4 bridges. Its wooded gorge provides sylvan walks. These are Durham's distinctive bounty in all seasons of the year, the rock & the river its gratuitous bonus.

sunshine on my favourite bridge crossing from trees to trees. W. Scott's verse SW end

A most impressive interior to sit & contemplate. St Cuthbert's tomb; Venerable Bede's tomb; Galilee Chapel; Treasury treasures; Neville Screen; Cosin Font; the Clock etc

ST· NICHOLAS CHURCH

3RD MARQUIS, LONDONDERRY BOTH IN CENTRAL MARKET PLACE

SILVER STREET TO CASTLE SADDLER STREET TO ELVET BRIDGE FLESHER GATE

Hilly town, steps up steps down.

Durham has also, of course, its Castle, its University, many interesting churches, Museums, good pedestrian ways, & the charms of sequestered precincts.

1832 FAMOUS BLACK TEAPOT, TRADE SIGN OF C19 GROCERS

KINGSGATE BRIDGE APPROACHES CATHEDRAL FROM THE EAST

BOATS IN SEASON

ELVET BRIDGE 1160 Old houses at its E·end, & summer boating of course

FOOTBRIDGE ACROSS GORGE, USED SPECIALLY BY STUDENTS.

THE WALLED CITY OF YORK

SEVERAL SHORT VISITS BETWEEN TRAINS ARE APPETISINGLY BUILDING FOR ME, A PICTURE OF YORK, IN EXCESS OF WHAT 2 PAGES CAN HOLD.

After the MINSTER, [splendid in its pinnacled twin towers & richly surfaced west front; in its most distinguished Chapter House (13 cusped, canopied, sculptured stalls, & what a roof! & in its figure sculptured Choir screen; in its remarkable Seven Sisters Window & a great deal else beside the (7 Crypt;----] THE WALLS were my next curiosity & enthusiasm.

Dear precious October day. Sunny. Still. Not a leaf moving. Gold in the trees. Gold under the trees. Fresh leafy carpets reflecting the sun. Such a day for looking, for gloating, for wondering. Sketch pad of course in hand, picnic in pocket.

YORK MINSTER

One can scrutinise the intricacies of the W. front ad infinitum. How many finial crosses on the buttresses? See the figure sculpture.

BOOTHAM BAR NORTH GATE

Up the steps of Bootham Bar we climbed in July sun, to glory in the high level views from ramparts & bastions, just as far as Jewbury today [noting the Ice House, & with a promise to complete the 2+mls of WALLS & 4 GATES at a later date.]

CARVED CAPITAL NORMAN CRYPT

Today, an August train break gave us [after a picnic by the Ouse] a gentle wander via the Herbert Read Arts Centre, & along King's Staithe to the Castle Folk Museum. Later, via ancient streets evocative names! to the fine Art Gallery, & Yorkshire Museum.

ON THE WALLS, THE PASSAGE NARROWS JUST HERE

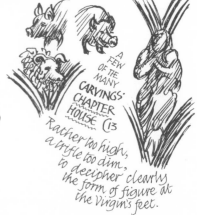

A FEW OF THE MANY CARVINGS. CHAPTER HOUSE (13 Rather too high, a trifle too dim, to decipher clearly the form of figure at the Virgin's feet.

THE PLEASANT RIVER WALK ALONG FROM LENDAL BGE TO OUSE BGE, GIVES VIEWS OF THE GUILDHALL

THIS CITY OF YORK

WHAT A TREASURE HOUSE!

RING HANDLE N. DOOR.

THE SIGHT OF THIS FILIGREE LANTERN, RISING ABOVE ROOFS IS CAPTIVATING & EXQUISITE. ALL SAINTS PAVEMENT CHURCH

St Martins & other fine old churches listed for next main break

NORTH BASTION

Different levels along THE WALLS so, frequent steps up & down

MONK BAR & THE GUARDIANS ON THE TOWER

OF THE 4 BARS THIS ONE IS N-E ENTRY

23 steps down to street level, here; 32 up, there; now 38 down! "Good exercise" I thought.

W. MULTIANGULAR TOWER

THE ONLY REMAINS OF MANY TOWERS OF DEFENCE ④ BRICK & STONE

IN MUSEUM GARDENS

ST MARY'S ABBEY

BENEDICTINE C4

REMAINS OF NAVE NOW A SETTING FOR YORK MYSTERY PLAYS

FOLK MUSEUM OF YORK THIS SIGN POINTS THE WAY PAST CLIFFORDS KEEP

CASTLE MUSEUM 1780   1705

CLIFFORD'S TOWER MEDIEVAL KEEP

ORIGINALLY THESE BUILDINGS WERE PRISONS

A TINY PLAN SHOWING GROUP OF BUILDINGS W. OF KINGS STAITHE

The sign board above, reminds me to mention the WHITE HORSE 15 mls N. of YORK, on HAMBLEDON HILLS to the E. WATCH ON THE RETURN JOURNEY.

Another vision! THE MINSTER TWIN TOWERS, glorious above Petergate

Sculptured MINERVA reclines against books above a CORNER SHOP in PETERGATE

THE WELL KNOWN SHAMBLES BUTCHERS QUARTER I like the wide window sills, & street gutters

Riverside walks & Boating here.

THE COBBLED QUAYSIDE OF KING'S STAITHE BY THE KING'S ARMS INN — LOOKING TOWARD SKELDERGATE BRIDGE

A SPLENDID CANOPY. WORTH MORE THAN THE GLANCE I GAVE IT

HERALDRY IN SCROLL IRONWORK

Some Rly glamour still left

YORK RLY STATION A little sketch as joyful evidence of waiting a few minutes until my train arrived dead on time.

SELBY ABBEY

THE TRAINS I USE NEVER STOP HERE, BUT I ALWAYS [ABOUT 12 MLS S. OF YORK] LOOK W. FOR THE MAJESTIC TOWERS of SELBY ABBEY "PLEASE VISIT HERE ALSO" THEY INSIST. A JOY IN STORE

LINCOLN MINSTER

I approached by rail, witnessing this amazing sight, this beacon of three jubilant, lofty & stately pinnacled towers, rising gloriously from an isolated hill; spectacular, unforgettable! Magnificent W. Front; triple transepts; Chapter Hse; Cloisters; richly faced porches; distinguished Angel choir; & much more, gave us to pause.

Intimate carved details caught my eye:- the W. Front; [Noah & Daniel,] the endearing Pilgrim; the Imp Tournai Font; Bosses; Misericords etc, [being once a stone carver myself]

PILGRIM

NORWICH CATHEDRAL

The Spire, the Tower, what refined perfection! Viewed from the wide cloisters, this purity gave such a lift to my heart that I forgot to draw the W. Front. The rounded Norman Apse, sublime from within & without. Can there be elsewhere such an enchanting & naïve collection of roof bosses? Misericords interesting also.

I'd like to learn these Cathedrals by heart, as one learns a poem.

BAPTISM

ROOF BOSS

BEVERLEY MINSTER

I had the luck to be in Beverley for 2 sunny hrs; made a beeline for the Minster & was knocked back by the magnificence & richness of the tall slender Highgate Porch facing North; unexpected, surprising, unique. Then, turning the corner, was again astonished by the soaring & lavish twin towers gilded by low winter sunshine. Inside, riveted by the label stop sculptures of Musicians, I gave scant attention elsewhere, & left, longing for a 2nd visit at ease, to Town as well as Minster.

HIGHGATE PORCH

CENTRAL SQUAT TOWER

WHAT IN BUTTRESSES

WHAT CONFIDENCE

WHAT PANACHE!

THESE MUSICIANS — ARE A FEAST OF VISUAL IMAGERY

ELY CATHEDRAL OF THE FENS,

in its stocky & robust grandeur dominates the Fens for miles around.

The N.W. Tower fell C15. Taking our picnic on Palace Green, we mourned its loss. Inside, we trained binocs on sculptured corbels; spotted the 2 imps; noted the inside outside clock; visited the Galilee Porch & Chantries; studied closely the Prior's Door & Stained Glass Exhibition.

OCTAGON LANTERN, ELY

What a rich, exquisite, beautiful & masterly centre piece this octagon lantern, rising from the crossing. [REMEMBER, 64' TREES MADE IT POSSIBLE]

A SINGLE PAGE CANNOT BE BUT A MEMENTO. NOTES & DRAWINGS OF EXTERNAL CONTOURS ONLY, IGNORING RICHES WITHIN. HOW TO APPORTION ONE PAGE IN FAIR MEASURE WAS A PROBLEM. THESE PRECIOUS, REMARKABLE, IRREPLACEABLE STRUCTURES, TODAY, LEAVE ONE STAGGERED AT THE SKILL, KNOWLEDGE, CONFIDENCE OF THE BUILDERS. SCULPTORS CERTAINLY ENJOYED FULL EMPLOYMENT!

PETERBOROUGH

JUST AN INTRODUCTORY ACQUAINTANCE ON THIS OCTOBER DAY.

No room on 1 page to draw "dandelion clock" fountains of Queen's Gate Centre, or Theatre on River Nene, or Cathedral Precincts, or Old Scarlet, or the landscaped environment, etc.

I have omitted BELL TOWER TURRETS rising from N·W. nave

Drawing one marvels at the rich embroidery of this great portal

MUST HAVE WESTERLY SUN FOR NEXT VISIT

BOSS IN C14 PORCH I had to try examining it against odds.

How benign these seated figures look

MONKS' OR HEDDA'S STONE CARVED, CHRIST & APOSTLES & SAXON MOTIFS (8 or 6) CURIOUS, & INTRIGUING

CATHEDRAL WEST FRONT

How daring, this vast, powerful triple portal, beneath the three enriched gables

A visual shock among cathedrals of Britain, & one recalls the cavernous facades of the Mosques of Central Asia etc.

Inside, a dead level floor from W·to·E· & great Barnack stone columns ascending with mighty strength to the fine timber ceilings [MARY Q·OF SCOTS WAS ORIGINALLY BURIED HERE]

The lively E·end with roundels & figure sculptures

Rounded corner towers, battlement tops S·TRANSEPT

Here a sun warmed seat in the cloister, [with a sandwich] gave a pause for the contemplation of this mighty work

LOOK UP! VERY RARE

PAINTED TIMBER CEILING 1220 NAVE

LOOK UP AGAIN!

PRESBYTERY VAULT IN TIMBER

Both repay the closest inspection. Binoculars? Mirror?

Tourism Centre, and a most obliging assistant, here in the TOWN HALL, BRIDGE ST WITH TOWER & 4 COLUMNED PORCH

FILIGREE CABINET IN CARVED BONE

A PRECIOUS POSSESSION

EXQUISITE WORK IN STRAW & BONE BY FRENCH PRISONERS (19 AT NORMAN CROSS, IS SHOWN IN THE MUSEUM & ART GALLERY, PRIESTGATE

C17 GUILDHALL & BUTTER MARKET, STURDILY PILLARED, & WITH TWIN SPIRAL STAIRCASES.

I'd like to give a whole day to wrestling with the perspective of a pierced metal spiral stair

IN THE CITY OF LONDON

SOME OF THE MORE INTIMATE DETAILS *lightly sketched*

THE GEORGE INN

CITY OF LONDON ... GRYPHON ON LONDON BGE & FLEET ST.

FUN CARVINGS [WOOD] GEORGE INN FLEET ST

As a memento I felt compelled to sketch these jolly works.

WIG & PEN CLUB 1625 FLEET ST

YE OLDE COCK TAVERN FLEET ST

CLUSTERED LAMPS OPPOSITE LAW COURTS & vaguely descried, the STATUE OF DR. JOHNSON

A most engaging sight, from Australia Hse SPIRES OF THE LAW COURTS, ST CLEMENT DANES, GLADSTONE STATUE, ALDWYCH. all among the trees.

I wonder what dreaming travesties I may have committed

Grasshopper, seal of Greshams, who founded the Bourse GRASSHOPPER VANE ROYAL EXCHANGE.

BEATEN COPPER CARAVEL 1895 ASTOR'S HSE

A tiny snowy feather came drifting down thro' FLEET ST

PATER NOSTER
by ELIZABETH FRINCK unveiled by YEHUDI MENUHIN

ST. BARTHOLOMEW THE GREAT CHANCEL

13 GILDED LIONS ON BLACK IRON PALINGS LAW SOCIETY CHANCERY LANE

consistent arcaded pattern of the Norman Choir was my first architectural thrill.

Having left the scene with my sketch, I always

IN DRY DOCK THE CUTTY SARK · R·NAVAL COLLEGE · QUEEN'S HSE · TOWER OF LONDON · LONDON BRIDGE · S·WARK CATH · MONUMENT · ST·PAUL'S CATHEDRAL

IN SEQUESTERED BACKWATERS among blackbirds, magpies, rooks, bluetits, robins. & drifting leaves of OCTOBER

IN LONDON

IN KEW GDNS

ONCE THE MOST MAGICAL THING IN MY YOUNG LIFE OF TWELVE YEARS

PAGODA 10 STOREYS

PITCHER PLANT

He made friends during my picnic

I searched out a picnic retreat in Lincolns Inn Fields. The more I looked up, the more of these curious animal terminals I saw between leaves of poplars, planes, mulberries, acacias.

PANOPLY OF LILIES. [IRONWORK] ALONG BREWSTER SCREEN. 4 OF THEM. LINCOLN'S INN F.

Behind Fleet St is the TEMPLE ROUND CHURCH with fine Norman Doorway, 60 carved grotesque heads, C13 Effigies, Font, striking arcading Purbeck marble piers.

One can take a pleasant contemplative seat in FOUNTAIN CRT, TEMPLE BAR

TWIN SPIRAL STAIRCASES IN THE PALM HOUSE

WHITE HORSE OF HANOVER

DRAGON OF WALES

YALE OF BEAUFORT

GREYHOUND OF RICHMOND

THE QUEENS BEASTS ARE NOW ALL DISPLAYED IN KEW GARDENS

FLORENCE NIGHTINGALE
1820 1910

ABRAHAM LINCOLN
1809 1865

SCULPTURE ABOVE POOL IN THE GARDEN OF ST PAUL'S CATHEDRAL

We gave our combined weight to the camels' humps for a spell of reverie on this unique seat, Victoria Embankment, this hot July day.

DISCOVERY • ST MARTIN LUDGATE • ST MARY LE BOW • ST BRIDE • POST OFF. TOW. • ST CLEMENT DANES • ST MARY STRAND • ST MARTIN FIELDS • CLEO NYLE • NELSON MON. • WESTMINSTER ABBEY • PALACE OF WESTMINSTER • VICTORIA TOWER • PARLIAMENT • BIG BEN •

Said Dr Johnson 1770, "When a man is tired of London he is tired of life, for there is in London all that life can afford."

Shelley declared:- "Hell is a city much like London. in 1820 A populous and smoky city".

Emerson observed, 1860, "London is the epitome of our times, & the Rome of today."

And what of *our* day? Chacun à son goût.

BEEFEATER

LORD MAYOR OF LONDON

WHITTINGTON SIR RICHARD WHITTINGTON THRICE LORD MAYOR OF LONDON

ONE OF LONDON'S BOBBIES

THE FAT BOY OF PIE CORNER THE GREAT FIRE WAS HALTED HERE GILTSPUR ST 1666

VETERAN CHELSEA PENSIONER

NOV 81, £1 TO ANYWHERE

On a train journey, S·C·TICKET, I revel in the interval of belonging neither here, nor there. In repose, I watch the landscape slide by, or dive into a book, or slay a crossword, or nibble a picnic, or muse & doze; or let the diversity of wheel music wash over me with a rumble & grumble, drone & moan, murmur & purr, slide & glide, shudder & shake; roar or scream or whistle; & all that, threaded with the diversity of chat & giggle & laughter from deep base to piping treble, over tones, undertones in a thorough going train orchestration.

THE RAIL JOURNEY'S END MEANS, "STIR YOURSELF, FOR THE RESPITE IS OVER. TAKE UP THE REINS YOU MUST."

SHAKY TRAIN

TRAIN PASSENGERS SPRING 1983

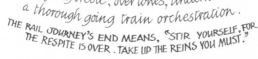

TRAIN TRAVELLERS 1971

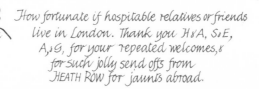

How fortunate if hospitable relatives or friends live in London. Thank you H&A, S&E, A,&G, for your repeated welcomes, & for such jolly send offs from HEATH ROW for jaunts abroad.

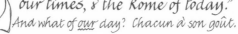

CHARLES DICKENS 1812-70

DR. JOHNSON 1709-84

A VISIT TO ANDALUCIA SPAIN FEB 1983

SNOWFLAKES

A FEW HOURS IN TORREMOLINOS MALAGA

Brilliant sun, biting wind. Walk & picnic near beach.

What is behind those canvas windbreaks?

Scorched bodies !!

Joining in? Simply appropriate a mattress. Divest. Fry the front. Turn over. Fry the back. Repeat. Pay when required.

Fish & tempting sea food & salad kept cool with fountain sprays

(MALAGA)

The Mediterranean here in Torremolinos: Tides? barely. Rocks, rock pools? No!

Gulls, gannets cormorants, duck? I saw none. No chorus, chanting, chatter, cackle, clamour, calling, cooing or carolling of sea birds. No.

But bougainvillea cascading, Dimorphotheca resplendent, Red hot pokers climbing cliffs, Mimosa, Geranium, Yellow oxalis & a still, waveless, tempting blue sea, too cold to try as yet.

Dear H & E,

Here is the illustrated letter you asked for, giving just the barest flavours of our richly packed visits hereabout.

You will be thinking of us under blue skies in brilliant powerful sunshine. Yes, but what a wind! It is keen & bitter, so be wary when choosing a picnic spot.

But would you imagine frost? snow? We've had both, & have driven through snowflakes, seen olive trees snow laden, firs like Christmas trees, icicles hanging from myrtle & mimosa.

Would you imagine clouds, rain, & mist? We've had very grey days, & sometimes rainy, dim afternoons, a mixter maxter of weather keeping us on tip toe & alert to seize sunshine & 'make hay', blessing our good luck, never a grumble if otherwise, & always good cheer from my most desirable companion, E. O. G.

We came specially to see the Moorish Palaces & Castles, [SEE OVER] to enjoy the spectacular colours & extravagancies of craftsmanship in arabesque, filigree, inlay; to see fountains & water gardens.

"The eye delights to trace unusual things
And deviates from the plain & common way."

The last Mosques I visited were in Istanbul 32 yrs ago.

Here, [as you can imagine knowing us,] no minaret goes unclimbed. "THE ONE ABOVE SEES ALL" & from the tops we read the pattern of life below as in the pages of a book; a landscape of tawny tiled roofs, patios, squares, parks; cypresses round the Mosque, & a ring of tower blocks girdling each city.

If you come next February be sure to bring winter woollies especially needed for sightseeing & high towers, also binoculars. And may you too enjoy – apart from the Spanish food – the bountiful oranges, heavy with sweet juice [almost given away,] & taste also the other mouthwatering fruits & vegetables displayed in markets.

Imagine the streets & squares of central Seville lined with picture book orange trees, dark green & hung with brilliant fruit, like gay baubles. These are the marmalade oranges soon to become British breakfast table conserve. [N.B. IN SEVILLE A WARNING ABOUT THE SCOURGE OF PICKPOCKETS, PROMPTED SAFE CUSTODY FOR PASSPORTS & TRAVELLERS CHEQUES.]

A billowing bountiful profusion of cascading potted plants from walls, window sills, patios, & balconies. LAVISH LARGESSE!

Each city has its wide boulevards & fountains, also its old quarter where, in the narrow alleys, immaculate white walls are spaced with balconies cascading foliage & flowers [pretty pink ivy geraniums blossoming now,] pot bellied iron grilles & ironwork lamps. Thro' open doors you can spy the tiled patios, arcaded & bright with potted plants, polished copper, colourful Hispano*Moresque plates, & filigree lanterns, all impeccably kept.

MANY SLEEK CATS ABOUT BUT NOT ALL IN ONE SPOT!

Driving the countryside, leaving the coastal sugar cane, & winding up to cross the craggy granite Sierra Nevada, we saw signs of Spring in flowering cherries, almonds, & carpets of iris histroides. The rolling treeless hill country beyond, was spotted with wells & growing melons, chick peas, lentils, asparagus etc & the ubiquitous olives. All this in country which absentee landlords had, previously allowed to become desert. Today, again the olive trees were white with snow above their little brown mats of earth, firs were Christmas trees, & icicles hung from myrtle & mimosa.

WHAT BASKETRY, THESE PANNIERS!

YOKED OXEN

In these parts one thinks of Columbus, Murillo, Don Juan, Don Quixote, Washington Irving, philosopher Maimonides, Seneca, & FLAMENCO! etc. [In the Victoria & Albert Museum, I always enjoyed the H.M.* ceramics & was intrigued by the name. Here it is prolific, even as graceful finial roof urns, & garden seats.] I will let you know how we spend our remaining few days – Gipsy Flamenco? – & shall enclose some further jottings which may perhaps sometime be of interest if you decide to go. With all best wishes to you, D. [£1 = 196 pesetas]

PRIEST

A TOTALLY BLACK FIGURE PENITENT OF SEVILLE. EASTER

IN SEVILLE
A FEW MEMORIES

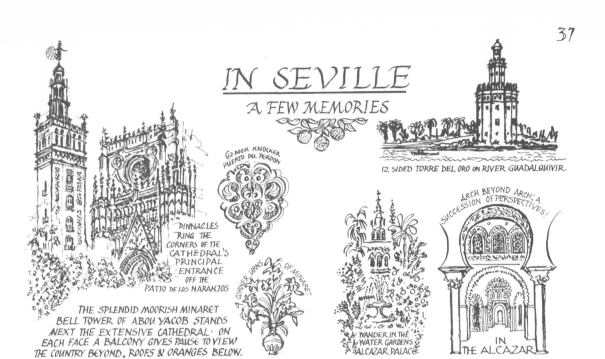

12 SIDED TORRE DEL ORO ON RIVER GUADALQUIVIR

12 DOOR KNOCKER PUERTO DEL PERDON

PINNACLES RING THE CORNERS OF THE CATHEDRAL'S PRINCIPAL ENTRANCE OFF THE PATIO DE LOS NARANJOS

A CORNER URNS OF MINARET

THE SPLENDID MOORISH MINARET BELL TOWER OF ABOU YACOB STANDS NEXT THE EXTENSIVE CATHEDRAL· ON EACH FACE A BALCONY GIVES PAUSE TO VIEW THE COUNTRY BEYOND, ROOFS & ORANGES BELOW.

WANDER IN THE WATER GARDENS ALCAZAR PALACE·

ARCH BEYOND ARCH· A SUCCESSION OF PERSPECTIVES!

IN THE ALCAZAR

We frequently hopped on buses [25p any journey,]. We sat in the Patio de los Naranjos, recalling "The Barber" Rossini & "Carmen" Bizet & contemplating the Giralda Tower with its 'statue of Faith' windvane & its 4 urns of lilies. Later we of course climbed its sloping ramp with dark spooky corners.....
We visited the huge richly decorated Cathedral. We admired the Alcázar Palace & enjoyed its garden retreat. We wandered the tangle of narrow white walled lanes of the Santa Cruz [potbellied iron grilles, flowery balconies, wall lamps]. We found our way down Boulevards to walk the river promenade under the Torre del Oro, river navigable to sea-going ships. Persistent cold demanded coffee brandies· Maria Louisa Park took us to the dignified arc of Plaza de España with its 5 bridges, splendid twin towers & outdoor museum in ceramics.
Of course much more than these [& Flamenco] can be enjoyed here in Seville.

SUPERB TAILORING FRILLS FOR THE FLAMENCO DANCE & FURBELOS

IN AMERICAN SQUARE (FAIENCE) CERAMIC PICNIC TABLE & ARMCHAIRS·

LOTS OF MOSAIC PAVEMENTS. HERE, FEATHERED BRICKWORK, PEBBLES, BLACK WHITE AND COLOURED. ALCAZAR PATIO.

THE SPACIOUS PLAZA DE ESPANA ALL MOSAIC TILED
A COMPLETE & SPLENDID ARCHITECTURAL CONCEPT·

PLAZA DE ESPANA IN CERAMIC BALUSTER

FINIAL

FOR EACH BRIDGE 2 PAIRS OF SLENDER STYLISH LAMPS PLAZA DE ESPANA

We climbed the Minaret seen here [tho' too large!] between orange trees of the Barrio Judería... A pity that I've drawn the tower quite out of proportion.

We had snowflakes y rain, saw storks gliding y one glued to the pinnacle of the Cathedral. Also saw the sad twisted lamps of the Plaza de los Dolores.

Our introduction to Cordoba, was a coche caballo drive, well blanketted against cold. A touristy gimmick, but great fun on this day of carnival when all were gay y costumed.
PLAZA DE JOSÉ ANTONIO.

CORDOBA SOME VIGNETTES

STUCCO ORNAMENT IN THE RARE FAMOUS & LOFTY C14 SYNAGOGUE WITH HEBREW INSCRIPTIONS ONLY 1 OTHER IN SPAIN, THAT IS IN TOLEDO.

FLOWERY PATIO. PRIDE OF THE HOME, AND SPOTLESSLY KEPT. PAVED & TILED, ADORNED WITH URNS, CERAMIC PLATES, POTS IN TRIPODS, IRON FILIGREE LAMPS, & CASCADING FLOWERS. ANNUAL COMPETIONS HELD. * *

A FEW DETAILS FROM THE MESQUITA *

WHAT AN EXTRAORDINARY BUILDING. A FOREST OF COLUMNS, 850, OF ONYX, MARBLE, JASPER GRANITE, SUPPORT A DOUBLE ARCHED CANOPY, RED & WHITE.

IN THE MIDDLE INTRUDES, LIKE AN EGG TOO BIG FOR ITS NEST, A LOFTY & HEAVY BAROQUE CATHEDRAL, CHARLES V. job!

PATTERNED VOUSSOIRS OF DOORWAY · MIHRAB.

THE MIHRAB, SEEN BETWEEN COLUMNS OF THE SCALLOPED ARCADED SCREEN LOOKS HEAVENLY & SACRED.

THE POSITION USUALLY CHOSEN FOR THIS SHRINE INDICATES THE DIRECTION OF MECCA

A FEW OF. THE MANY WALL ENRICHMENTS

SUGGESTING FLOWERS, FOLIAGE

I liked his sensitive face y hands, y moccasins polished by fingering.
MAIMONIDES Jewish Philosopher
Seated statue

'HORSE SHOE' ARCH OF ENTRANCE E. FACADE MESQUITA

INSET ABOVE FOILED ARCADE · WHAT A DEAL OF SKILL & SCHEMING HERE!

STORKS, FISH BY THE OLD ARAB MILLS NEXT THE DEAR OLD ROMAN BRIDGE.

I enjoyed the gentle slope downhill thro' the town to the river.

A REMINDER OF CURIOUS INTERLACING. WALL ARCADE.

THE ALHAMBRA PALACE

of *Granada* is to me

a name pregnant with magic & allure.
There it stands, a walled retreat of trees,
of towers & courts, set apart on its spacious green
cliff high above the busy city, its backcloth the snowy
shining summits of the lofty Sierra Nevada range.
WHAT A GRAND SPECTACULAR SETTING!

THE HILL ROCK· PALACE RINGED WITH OUTER TOWERS, WALLS, DEFENCES.

"The splendour falls on castle walls
And snowy summits old in story"
In the bewitching light of sunset
I recalled Tennyson's lines.

Climb up. Enter. Slowly wander your way
through pavilions & patios; courts,
cloisters, halls & marble baths
with perfumed perforations.

Slender columns;
Scalloped arcades;
painted & panelled
inlaid ceilings;
coffered stalactite domes;
walls enriched with
pierced intricacies of
arabesque, filigree, interlace,
& peppered with inscriptions;
floors of marble, tile, inlay,
of tinkling fountains
cooling water runnels,
& art that conceals art.

PATIO DE LOS LEONES
Delicately ethereal
Substance? Dream? Music? Poetry?

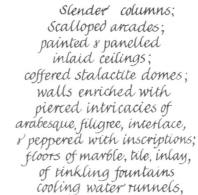

HONEY COMB CORBELS WITH SCALLOP SHELL HOODS

ARABIAN NIGHTS TALES C15 C16 cf. WASHINGTON IRVING 1783–1859

PIERCED FILIGREE WINDOW

CARVED MOTIFS, STUCCO, FESTOON WALLS
SEE POMEGRANATES

Such indulgent richness! A visual feast of wonder
& enchantment. Views below & beyond make it all an
intoxicating experience & our 3 visits were far too few.

WALLS ARE BOOKS TO BE READ

TO DRAW IS TO EXAMINE MORE CLOSELY, BUT—
SO MUCH TO SEE, NO TIME EVEN TO SKETCH,
BAR THE MEREST THUMBNAIL FRAGMENTS.
SO MUCH BEAUTY, BUT OH! THE OTHER SIDE OF THE COIN—
CONSPIRACY, INTRIGUE, SPILT BLOOD, ASSASSINATION !!!!

THE OPEN HAND SIGNIFIES
5 PRECEPTS OF THE KORAN
BELIEF IN THE ONENESS OF GOD,
FASTING,
PRAYER,
ALMSGIVING,
PILGRIMAGE.

Keystone PORTO OF JUSTICE

ALLAH ALONE IS VICTORIOUS OVER ALL

THE GENERALIFE GARDEN
ALHAMBRA PALACE FEB. '83

"Flowers are to a garden
As stars to the sky."

On no account miss this garden. "GENERALIFE" means Garden of Architects. These buildings are white, Palace buildings red.

From this hill near the Palace see the caves which riddle the opposite hillside.

They've sheltered in turn early Christians, Visigoths, Moors & now Gypsies.

This garden makes the garden look mild. Joseph Brian Feb 16

My image was quite eclipsed by the reality of this airy garden retreat set along the hillside.

Terraces climb the hill tier upon tier cypress hedged, cypress arched, mosaic paved, bedded & urned.

FLORAL MOSAIC PAVED GARDEN WALK UNDER WISTARIA

You come upon arbours, nooks, shaded walks, wide vistas, dark stepways, arcaded pavilions, & still, reflecting pools, shot with darting goldfish. But the fountains, how they intrigued me! Variously grouped jets play tunes with crystal drops, & waterfalls splash from level to level. All this water is powered by those eternal snows of the Sierra Nevada mountains.

SALTAMONTES
THIS VEGETARIAN WAS LIFTED FROM THE WIDE HARD PAVING

"Water is the Mother of Earth
And plants are her Children."

Myrtle mimosa, magnolia, orange, oleander, cedar, cypress, yew, plane, palm etc punctuate the background of courts cloisters & pavilions.

AN OPEN
POMEGRANATE-GRANADA'S SYMBOL

Flowers will shortly blossom to paint the borders & waft their perfumes across the oval theatre where many artists, Margot Fonteyn & Nureyev, Segovia & others have entranced audiences in still, cool, fragrant evenings, when;-

FOUNTAIN PERSPECTIVE OF LONG POOL.

3 FLOORS SHOWING THE BALCONIES OF HOTEL LOS ANGELES, LOOKING ABOVE, ALONG, & DOWN; BELOW TO POOL & ACROSS TO SNOWY PEAKS, SIERRA NEVADA.

"Now sleeps the crimson petal, now the white
Nor waves the cypress in the palace walk
Nor winks the gold fin in the porphyry font..."
ALFRED TENNYSON 1809 - 1892

MUSICAL TINKLING OF MANY WATER JETS IN GOLDFISH & LILY POOLS

Today we irreverently took our picnic in the theatre here.

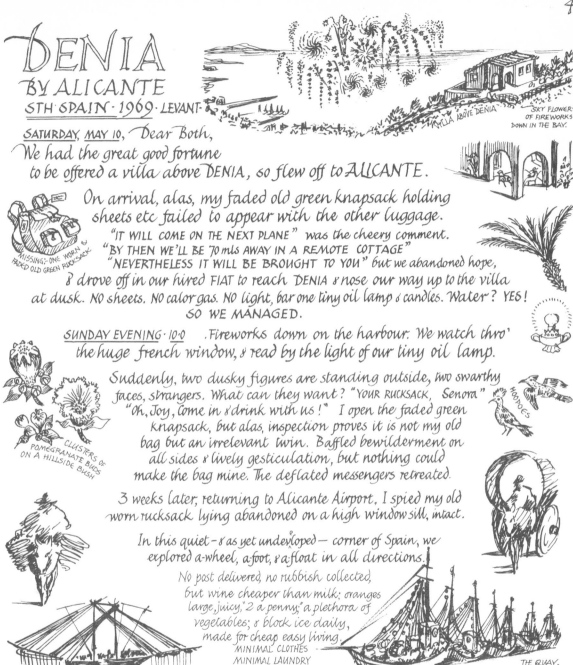

DENIA
BY ALICANTE
STH SPAIN · 1969 · LEVANT·

VILLA ABOVE DENIA

SKY FLOWERS OF FIREWORKS DOWN IN THE BAY.

SATURDAY, MAY 10, Dear Both,

We had the great good fortune to be offered a villa above DENIA, so flew off to ALICANTE.

On arrival, alas, my faded old green knapsack holding sheets etc failed to appear with the other luggage.

MISSING:- ONE WORN & FADED OLD GREEN RUCKSACK

"IT WILL COME ON THE NEXT PLANE" was the cheery comment. "BY THEN WE'LL BE 70 mls AWAY IN A REMOTE COTTAGE" "NEVERTHELESS IT WILL BE BROUGHT TO YOU" but we abandoned hope, & drove off in our hired FIAT to reach DENIA & nose our way up to the villa at dusk. NO sheets. NO calor gas. NO light, bar one tiny oil lamp & candles. Water? YES! SO WE MANAGED.

SUNDAY EVENING · 10·0 . Fireworks down on the harbour. We watch thro' the huge french window, & read by the light of our tiny oil lamp.

CLUSTERS OF POMEGRANATE BUDS ON A HILLSIDE BUSH

Suddenly, two dusky figures are standing outside, two swarthy faces, strangers. What can they want? "YOUR RUCKSACK, Senora" "Oh, Joy, Come in & drink with us!" I open the faded green knapsack, but alas, inspection proves it is not my old bag but an irrelevant twin. Baffled bewilderment on all sides & lively gesticulation, but nothing could make the bag mine. The deflated messengers retreated.

HOOPOES

3 weeks later, returning to Alicante Airport. I spied my old worn rucksack lying abandoned on a high window sill, intact.

In this quiet - & as yet undeveloped — corner of Spain, we explored a-wheel, a-foot, & a-float in all directions.

No post delivered, no rubbish collected, but wine cheaper than milk; oranges large, juicy, "2 a penny;" a plethora of vegetables; & block ice daily, made for cheap easy living. MINIMAL CLOTHES MINIMAL LAUNDRY MINIMAL HOUSEWORK.

THE QUAY, DESERTED; ONLY US HERE, FOR, ON A QUIET SUNDAY, FLEET IN PORT

Cables fan out from the mast to booms. From these hang the lines for growing & catching mussels popularly used in paella.

From the cottage high above & 1 mile from coast we would hear the boats chug chugging on return with their catches. Then the Quay came alive with bidding & buying:- scallops, mussels, flounders prawns, crabs, mackerel etc. What a press & hubbub!!

But this holiday was an extra, for, we'd planned, *this same year* to use the £50 Statutory Travel Allowance for visiting friends in New York, Seattle, Canada, N.Zealand & N.S.Wales! Without broaching this nestegg, could we survive? A little scheming solved the problem :–

Ivory, waxy, Moon Flowers cascade across garden walls.

MAUVE SPIRES OF JACARANDA TREES

As usual, buy Travel tickets at home.
Also buy car hire at home.
Pack & take staple food, iron rations.
Use part sterling notes allowance, in Pesetas· £15.
Use overplus of car allowance, £25 weekly, in Pesetas.
& by these means, our modest needs were met.
£1 = 166 pesetas.
& this villa became home from home to us.
"Thank you, Liz & John."
I frequently repeated.

Our local, *stony* countryside grew :–
saxifrage, iris, garlic,
grape hyacinth, lavender,
poppy, fennel, achillea, sage,
rosemary, gladioli, lupin etc,etc.

OCTOPI SKINS PEGGED OUT TO DRY ON THE COAST

Deep fissures IN THE CLEFT ROCK; STEPS UP THROUGH ROCK ARCH TO CASTELLO & SCHOOL ON ITS CLIFF PERCH

BELFRY ON ITS OWN ROCK PINNACLE

STEEP, COBBLED STREETS, HOUSE FRONTS BUILT AGAINST VERTICAL ROCK WALLS

GUADALEST.
What a remarkable skyline of craggy turrets & pinnacles. Of all the rock landscapes here about, surely this is most staggering I recalled the Meteora [GREECE] & Erice [SICILY.]

A STOCK OF COUNTLESS POTTERY VESSELS WEATHERING ROUND ABOUT.

Away in the country, an old potter
works at his wheel, & slings his pots on lines, trees,
& tripods, two & three deep, right along the hillside. No wind? No rain?

FRIGHTENINGLY GROTESQUE
Nearby us,
Along the hillside among gnarled
olives, dark carob, & prickly pear, an old
peasant, now 80, has built a watch tower
for himself, surrounding it with a bizarre collection
of weighty spooky stone shapes, selected from the craggy hillside,
laboriously carried & set in position to make fantastic statuary groups.
A harmless cranky pleasure, but what a lark! An outdoor Museum.

Surely this must be DON QUIXOTE? or SANCHO PANZA?

MAY WE, ALL SEVEN OF US, IN OUR RETIREMENT, KEEP BUSY WITH PROJECTS & PLOYS HOWEVER ODD. With all good wishes, from D

A FEW DRAWINGS
& NOTES FROM
MY SKETCH DIARIES

HERE & THERE
IN ITALY
& ALPS

" Travelling is the ruin of all happiness! There's no looking at a building here after seeing Italy," wrote F. Burney 1810

"Let me/go where I will, I hear the sky born music still, And in the darkest meanest things There's always, always something sings" wrote R.W. Emerson 1870

THE GLEAMING WHITE MARBLE BELL TOWER OF COURSE WE CLIMBED, AND DREW FROM BELFRY

THE BAPTISTERY ✶ ✶ ✶ CAMPANILE   THE DUOMO·W FACADE

"I do not want Michael Angelo for breakfast, for luncheon, for dinner for tea, for supper, for between meals. Lump the whole thing! say the Creator made Italy from designs by Michael Angelo." wrote Mark Twain.

PISA. THE LEANING TOWER, DUOMO, OF COURSE. I WAS NOT PREPARED FOR SUCH A STUNNING SIGHT AS THIS, & OF SUCH MAGNITUDE; THESE 3 SHINING WHITE ARCADED BUILDINGS, RISING UNINTERRUPTED FROM THE BRIGHT GREENSWARD. GRAND, NOBLE, ELECTRIFYING·

While in Orkney & Shetland 1970, we frequently crossed paths of a foreign couple. They became interested in my sketches. We fraternised. Said they; "You're from Edinburgh, we are from Florence, two of the finest cities in Europe. We should exchange homes." Trustingly we did.

IN TUSCANY, 1971.

There they were, R & E, [foreign correspondents for Il Nazione] in PISA to welcome & waft us, first to their flat in Lido di Camaiore where they possessed a pitch on the beach.

BUT WE MUCH PREFERRED THE ALPI APUANE, THE HILL VILLAGES & TOWNS, THE MARBLE QUARRIES OF CARRARA, & THE GRAPE HARVEST OF THE CINQUE TERRA, ALL LYING HARD BY.

FROM TIME TO TIME, FOLK LEAVE THEIR PRIVATELY OWNED PITCH, TO TAKE A COOL CONSTITUTIONAL ALONG THE FRINGES OF THE SEA.

HEAT MIST VEILS ALPI APUANE RANGES.

ON THE BEACH

WE PREFER HILLS TO SAND UNDERFOOT

So, maps consulted, rare routes chosen & Renzo kindly drove us.

"Each district has its specialty" said Emilia, & insisted we should stop to taste:- Golfiotto; or Brigidine; or Moka; or Salami; or Pané di Altopascio; or Mescina, & other such local dishes. But what could excel fresh walnuts, figs, or luscious jade grapes picked from the vine?

CYCLAMEN ABOUND

GRAPE VINES.

How to convey their charm? Canopies, screens, arcades, pergolas, terraces of them. My Travel Journal is exultant. drawings flow. We were N. of Lerici (Shelley) & N. of La Spezia, in RIOMAGGIORE & MANOROLA.

GRAPE BASKETS UNDER FIG TREE ABOVE SEA

The CINQUE TERRA grape harvest sparkled. Terraced vineyards clothed the steep cliffs down to blue seas. Heat; sun, light, poured down. We lunched on the brink of a precipice under a spreading chestnut canopy.

Those hill villages, BARGA, COREGLIA, etc theatrical, a feast of viewing; & the marble quarrying unforgettable, dramatic.

THOUGHTS OF M. ANGELO; H. MOORE

LUCCA

Baffling maze of narrow streets Bel Paese & aniseed crisps

Remember wicker work market

Fortified brick built ramparts surround town, planted with pruned planes like candelabra. Under these, we took cheese, nut, grape picnic; Apuane Alps beyond.

CAPALETTA

Tilted, twisting stepped vennel up to Duomo. BARGA, ALPI APUANE

R & E were most generous hosts, distinctive in their warm friendliness & quality of living.

They now drove us [passing PUCCINI's villa] to become sole proprietors of their MILL on the ARNO. Then came the initiation.

20' high metal gates; heavy mediæval keys. Very tricky. The right key, the right number of turns, the right push & pull at the right moment & you were in. Next the great porch door. Electric locks combination locks had to be mastered. ONCE OUT SHOULD WE EVER GET IN, WE WONDERED.

WILL THE REALITY EQUAL THE PHOTOS, WE WONDER.

APPROACHING, OUR CURIOSITY LEAPT, OUR HEARTS BEAT FAST. EXCITEMENT, APPREHENSION. WHAT RESPONSIBILITY TO CARRY! WHAT FUN! 4 CATS.

MULINA
DI S. ANDREA A ROVEZZANO
THE LEFTMOST WING WAS OURS + TERRACE GARDEN
WITH VIEW ACROSS THE RIVER ARNO

MARBLE ENTRANCE HALL
WITH SPIRAL STAIRCASE

HANGING STAIR LAMP
SUSPENDED FROM
ROOF SKYLIGHT

WINDOW
GRILL
OF OUR
GROUND
FLOOR
BED
ROOM

On the walls of this vennel are scratched British names, for at this point in 1944, the Allied Army crossed the Arno, the enemy was routed & the Mill became British H.Q.

Renzo & Emilia showed us the ropes & door locking rituals, presented prosciuto, fettunta, finocchiona, chianti, & departed, leaving us trustingly in sole charge.

From this palatial home 4 mls up river from FLORENCE with its blissful garden looking on to the Arno, we once again took familiar ways in this loved city with much affectionate recall of April visits in '49 & '59, [recorded in earlier sketch books] when the city was quiet & tourists fewer. Very different now.

Revisiting, we were no less astonished than before, contemplating the great possessions of this city & felt further enriched — not least by the pastries delicatessen & fabulous ice creams.

R: had driven us in ALTO VERSILIA for the sunset from Montecatini, S·Lucia, & Montigiore, & now we were savouring countrysides of Fiesole, Vinci, San Gimignano Siena & the vineyards of Chianti, with always happy homecomings to the Mill. How could we bear to leave it? But October was running out. Our gratitude to the Cantagalli's is marked by truly unique memories, & a
FULL & LYRICAL TRAVEL JOURNAL.

DIOSPERI, PEARS, FIGS, WALNUTS, IN THE MILL GARDEN.

STROZZI PALACE FLORENCE
LINK HOLDER   ANGLE LANTERN

DUOMO, FLORENCE.
BIRDS FROM PANEL OF GHIBERTI'S BAPTISTERY DOOR

IN FLORENCE 1949
WITH SIGNORA MARIA CORRIDI·
MEMORIES OF 2, GIUSEPPE GIUSTI, & SHOP WINDOWS.

UFFIZI GALLERY '71
SPECTATORS

19
49

IN 1949 WE GLOATED, FEASTING OUR EYES ON FRILLY DRESSES, DELICATESSEN. WE YET FACED 4 LONG YEARS OF COUPONS & DOCKETS

A PAN OF FRIED EGGS WAS A RARE SIGHT TO RATION WEARY EYES.

OUR MEALS WERE SERVED BY WHITE GLOVED HANDS. FINGER BOWLS, ETIQUETTE, IN PERIOD PROPRIETY. A GRATIFYING NICETY.

FOR WAY OUT FASHION,

SEE NOT ONLY PAINTINGS, BUT

THE AVANT GUARDE SPECTATORS

A LOOK AT TUSCANY & UMBRIA 1959.

Dear R, & O,   March 1959

   Buongiorno!   Can you imagine us 4 ladies sardined in a new little hired Fiat? We drove from MILAN via BOLOGNA to FLORENCE thro' torrents of lashing rain; buckled the boot in a wild moment; climbed over the Apennines, Raticosa Pass, 3175 with headlights, & were very relieved to arrive safely in FLORENCE.

SUN FOR OUR DAYS THERE, & FOR THE WHOLE JOURNEY TO URBINO. EMPTY ROADS ALL THE WAY, & WE NEVER SPOTTED A SINGLE BRITISH CAR.

S. GIMIGNANO
2 OF ITS 13 TOWERS

What picnic lovers we are, & our "Volcano" a trusty stalwart for hot drinks, hot snacks. Chianti, cheeses, fruits etc from villages at hand, & always choice & delectable spots to hoard in our memories.
   My sketch book is full of them.

VOLCANO= DOUBLE CYLINDER; WATER JACKET ROUND CENTRAL CHIMNEY.

DRY TWIGS INTO FIRE BASKET: SOON FUNNEL STEAMS: & QUICK FRY ON EMBERS:

IN SIENA FINE ALTARPIECES. ART GALLERY.

Cyclamen, primroses, violets, grape hyacinth, alkanet hellebore, anemones, etc; breka kekek of countless frogs, blossoms opening as we watch, vine leaves breaking, evidence of Spring in green brilliance all around.

We walked the hilly campagna, sat by rivers with women swirling their laundry, the Metaurus gave thoughts of Hannibal & Co. We wrote, sketched, read, alfresco, ate trout from Lake Trasimene, polenta, pecorino; enjoyed dumb show & a nodding acquaintance with the local peasants. Sharp clefts of river valleys, cliffs & rocks, recalled the scenes in Early Tuscan & Umbrian genre paintings.

HILL TOP FARMS STACKS CUT TO CORE
SAN MARINO PEAK 15m AWAY

VINES

ANOTHER DELIGHTFUL PICNIC ZUPPA, UOVO FRITTATA PANE BURRO FORMAGGIO LATTE ARANCIA MELE CHIANTI

Our free Museum Passes were well used. Oh, the impact of those medieval towers of S. Gimignano, & the black & white Cathedral of SIENA! [liquorice allsorts we said] The Arezzo Frescoes, PIERO DELLA FRANCESCA, & PERUGIA'S remarkable Fountain in the central square etc are memorably special. ASSISI, stationed majestically on the hillside ahead, impressed so much that we parked the car to gaze, & took a picnic there, before proceeding to the Basilica

"Spring, the sweet Spring, is the year's pleasant king..." wrote T.Nash.1590

PERUGIA

ASSISI ON S.W. SIDE OF HILL OVER LOOKS THE PLAIN OF UMBRIA

FINE IRON WORK EVERY WHERE

CYCLAMEN

ALKANET

BASILICA, ST FRANCIS OF ASSISI

FROM TERRACE OF PALAZZO WE NOTICED 3 DISTINCT LEVELS OF STREETS; BDGS SILHOUETTED DRAMATICALLY AGAINST PLAIN BELOW, UMBRIAN HILLS BEYOND.

Then we crossed the Apennines on the tortuous climb over the Furlo Pass from Gubbio at dusk [mindful of the wolf] to land in URBINO by 8·30. Dinner tables & our rooms both graced with cyclamen.

I think you'd like Urbino. Unspoiled town, walled, with University; Ducal Palace; superb Art Gallery; Botanic Gdn; book shops galore [tho' not one in English] A prize retreat. No tourists, so we are cosseted in every way. Enticing surrounding country, hilly, flowery; sweet warm scent of bean fields. Please thank Charlotte for recommending.

These hill towns are all so very attractive we were loath to leave them, but now drove down to the plain, & raced along, crossing the Rubicon, to RAVENNA. My second visit, & the mosaics not one whit less magical, but even more enthralling to me than in 1953

Binoculars picked out the details in S·Vitale, S·Apollinare Nuovo, & in Classe:- sandals, stoles, lilies, & the portrait heads of the Baptistery cupola; but are not needed for the tiny mausoleum of Galla Placidia, where one steps from sunlight to darkness, & beauties are one by one revealed with intimate charm.

A landscape of blossoming orchards brought us to FERRARA, an arcaded city where we'd have liked a longer stay. Then after the EUGENIAN Hills, PADUA, but this time unfortunately the Scrovegni Chapel [GIOTTO FRESCOES] was closed.

Now for Venice. Shall we see you there? I know how partial you are to this Queen of cities. Best wishes to you for yr travels, from D.

URBINO seen after sunset [alfresco coffee] from Mausoleum of the Dukes, who were all patrons of the Arts. The Institute of Art deals specially with Book Production. 4,000 stud. in University. We enjoyed the markets. [This sketch is compressed left to right.]

CEILING OF RAPHAEL'S HOUSE

Gentle lady custodian, full of pride for this house.

HILL & MOUNTAIN VILLAGES HAVE REDUCED WOOD STACKING TO AN ART. TWIGS TO LOGS GRADED, MARSHALLED. M VERY INTRIGUED BY THIS

REED & TWIG BESOM, BOTANIC GARDEN.

URBINO IS SET ON A HILL WITH 2 HORNS FROM THE SQUARE, N & S· ROADS SLOPE DOWN, E & W RUN UPHILL. FAT PIGEONS NESTLED IN THE MASONRY NICHES UNDER MY WINDOW.

RAVENNA MOSAICS

LILIES IN S·APOLLINARE IN CLASSE

DONATELLO'S 'GATTAMELATA' PIGEON ON BOUND TAIL! [MY PADUA MEMENTO]

PENDANT LAMP MARKET ARCADE FERRARA

IN S. VITALE

COLOUR IS RICH

PATRICIAN LADY IN THEODORA'S RETINUE

S. VITALE BROOCH & SANDALS EMPEROR JUSTINIAN

IN S· VITALE

ARCADE IN FERRARA

NAVE FINIAL DUOMO FERRARA

THE UNDULATING UMBRIAN SKYLINES & TWISTING TRACKS GAVE EXULTANT WALKING

IN VENICE

With some trepidation we returned the Fiat in Mestre, confessed to the parking summons [most innocently collected,] & to the buckled boot. Both were waived with indulgent smiles, much to our relief, & we were forthwith driven to VENICE in style.

"See Naples & die" has been said,
We have seen it & lived on to visit
Pompeii & circle Vesuvius twice* from above.

"All roads lead to Rome" is also said.
Ours often has. But for me VENICE, the
island city, with sheer charm, leads the way.
Go in the quiet of the year
to enjoy its spell.

The matchless Basilica
its 4 horses & mosaics;
the 'fairy tale' Ducal Palace;
balconied palaces
rising from sparkling waters;

the network of canals;
graceful slender black gondolas;
lacy foot bridges humped
& approached by steps;
the singular, comely, Rialto bridge;

the Campanile & its bells;
fine churches;
Art Galleries:-

BELLINI, CRIVELLI, CARPACCIO,
GIORGIONE, TITIAN, TINTORETTO,
VERONESE, CANALETTO,
EXUBERANT TIEPOLO etc.

The Lagoon Islands;
Torcello Basilica;
Murano glass;
Burano lace.

SHOPS, MARKETS, BOATS,
ST. MARK'S SQ.
aperitif?
ices?
confections?

LUXURY GONDOLAS,

coal black, highly polished, shining brass fittings, carvings, scented roses in silver vase.

3 sterns with crocket finials

twisty rollocks & mooring poles.

GONDOLAS BOBBING ON THE WATER FRONT "black swans" & every bit as graceful

MY SKETCH DIARY SHOWS THIS BRUSHED IN.

Before zero hour for train home, I felt compelled to draw these soaring angel figures on skyline of S. Marco.

Here are 5 romantic scenes carved among acanthus leaves on the capital of a column in the arcade of the DOGE'S PALACE. What a sad anticlimax.

HALBERD BOWS OF GONDOLA

'BLACK SWANS'

Umbrella collisions common in narrow CALLE off S. Mark's Sq.
We had a downpour
ALL UMBRELLAS BLACK IN 1949

"AND HE SENT FORTH A RAVEN"

MOSAICS IN THE NARTHEX OF THE DUOMO

"AND HE SENT FORTH A DOVE"

MY MEMORY, EXPLORING IN VENICE, APRIL 20 1949

* Can you credit that in 1950 the air pilot offered this bonus sight?

SOME NOTES ON TRAVEL
"Away I'm bound to go"

<u>To where?</u> Friends? Relatives? Historic site? Cities? Beaches? Off the beaten track? On a spree? etc.
<u>How?</u> Rly train? Pleasure boat? Plane? Coach? Horse & carriage? shank's pony? 4 legged pony? Bike? rickshaw? etc?

"Go and catch a falling star" if you can. OR, Stay & enjoy arm chair travel, extensively, cheaply, & in comfort. A magic carpet will waft you anywhere, everywhere, with the aid of maps, books.

The best value in the world for money must be our 1955 journey Milan to Syracuse £3·6·0. The train ran on to the ferry for Sicily [SCYLLA & CHARYBDIS]. [At Milan crowds had swarmed on to the train & we took refuge in a reserved compartment to draw breath. Next minute we were locked in! The occupants never arrived. What roomy comfort for us!] The next best value is the TRANS CANADIAN RLY Roomette, but that later.

My Sicily Journal of 1955 advises:-

A CROSS COUNTRY LIFT FOR ME, THE OTHERS UNWILLING.

IN TRAIN PALERMO TO MESSINA

WATER FOUNTS ON RLY STATIONS IN ITALY

RAIN IN SYRACUSE, SICILY 1955

HAVE HANDY IN TRAIN :-
Air cushion, Toiletries, Bottle opener, cup, Waterbottle, [Water founts on stations] Tin opener, Iron rations, Snack food.

HAVE HANDY ON PLANE :-
Sun Specs, ear plugs, barley sugar, maps.

HAVE IN POCKET, HANDBAG :-
Passport, Tickets etc, Travellers cheques, Cash, F. currency in notes & change, Guide book, Phrase book, Note book & pencil.

ON APPROACHING NEXT CENTRE :-
Study map, for location of Rly Stn, Tourist Office, Travel Agent, Banks, Hostels etc.

NB Avoid Easter Monday travel. Passengers pay 15% supplement on Rapidos. Some Rapidos for 1st & 2nd class only, ∴ carry Time Table for reference. IIIrd class travel is cheap but crowded, so board at terminus if possible. For hard seats, air cushion. On night trains travel IInd for upholstered seats.

1949 WHAT BANANAS

IN CALAIS WE HAD NOT SEEN THEM FOR YEARS

WHITE CLIFFS OF DOVER FROM VICTORIA

ROCK & ROLL ACROSS CHANNEL

WRECKS STILL SHOWING ON DUNKIRK BEACHES APRIL 1949

NIGHT TRAIN HOURS. CALAIS, BASLE, ST GOTHARD, MILAN, PADUA.

POST PRANDIAL NAP

1953 3 RD CLASS. SLEEPING HARD YET THE DAY BROUGHT FUN WITH ITALIAN TROOPS. NB. TOM SLEPT ON LUGGAGE RACK

NORTH SEA

CROSSING

BREEZY, ON THE M.V. ETTRICK, LEITH, ROTTERDAM 1966

TURKISH CUSTOMS 1951 "WHAT JEWELLERY HAVE YOU"?

MEN ON LUCERNE BOAT 19.4.99.

ON BOAT, ATHENS-CRETE 1951

MILITARY GUARD BOSPOROUS, BLACK SEA BOAT. 1951

2 WHEELS BETTER THAN 4

TRAVEL IS ALL PART OF THE HOLIDAY

"IT IS BETTER TO TRAVEL THAN TO ARRIVE" R·L·S * DO YOU AGREE?

SAILING IN SYRACUSE FOR PAPYRUS

CHARACTERS, LUCERNE BOAT 16.4.49

ALPINE JOYS.

Alpine pastures, alpine villages, alpine valleys, lakes, streams, flowers, cowbells, lush meadows, snowy peaks, cable cars, ski slopes. What a dream world! We've revelled in its sport, its scenery, its people, the traditional hospitality, the food, the orderliness.

In the 1930's, I drank deep of the intoxicating ski slopes at Christmas & New Year. St Jacob am Arlberg was my centre.

We in our austerity & severe paper shortage, had forgotten such refinements by 1949!

After the war, Spring 1949 Beckenreid, Lake Lucerne, became my paradise. Lisa Rutiman, a friend indeed, most bountiful & indulgent. Perhaps war strains in London & Bristol, [fire watching, bombing, rationing] had taken their toll & we much appreciated many kindnesses;- bedroom breakfast tray, balcony lunch, dinner under Linden tree, etc. No car. Just legs, boats, bus, cable car. My sketch book is lyrical.

Fresh picked flowers on Lisa's charming breakfast tray. 1949

Daisy chains

Threading daisies on a green alp. What contrast to the fire watching '39-45 & extinguishing fire bombs.

1. Anna. 7.8 Geiferins
HAND PAINTED WARDROBE IN HOTEL B'ROOM
I returned home to paint my own one.

1966, OUR RETIREMENT YEAR.
Off we went, 3 of us, frolicking. Car this time. Leith, North Sea, Rotterdam, drive to Basle. Then potter off the beaten track. LIESBERG. What a find! Swiss Jura. Gasthaus in "village Square. Days of timeless pleasures, lily of valley, solomon's seal, WILD!

Then empty roads threading thro' pastures, dandelion fields sunny gold, villages of the EMMENTAL, Langnau, Napf, Ludenalp, Lucerne & GAIS. a most captivating centre.

IT IS IRREVERENTLY SAID:---
IN 6 DAYS, THE LORD MADE HEAVEN
& EARTH. ON THE SEVENTH HE WAVED
HIS WAND, & HEY PRESTO, GAIS APPEARED.

The Alpine way of draining WELLINGTONS

COW, GOAT, SHEEP BELLS

Every variety, small to large, with various tinklings

YODELLERS
PRACTISE AT SUNDOWN IN VILLAGE SQ.
FOR XAVIER'S 80th BIRTHDAY TRIBUTES

Emmenthal houses, tent roofs like wide protective skirts, hooded gables, cowled attics, balconied floors, fruit trees

We were uplifted, treading on air, & climbed Alps in all directions. Spent one idyllic day dallying on hillside, watching silver snows retreat from the slopes of SANTIS. [recorded with purple patches in my travel diary.]

COOLING SPRAY AT HORSE TROUGH

ANY BIRDS, MARMOTS, CHAMOIS, SKIERS, CLIMBERS, AVALANCHES?

Just 3 of the endless enjoyments that filled the fleeting days.

A LANDSCAPE OF GREEN HILLOCKS SCATTERED CHALETS & SKEINS OF TWISTING PATHS

OUR HOTEL GAIS IN FOUNTAIN SQ

COPSES FLING BLOCKS OF SHARP SHADOW DOWN HILLSIDES

A ROW OF COW PAINTINGS, RUNNING ALONG OUTSIDE WALL OF A COW SHED!

1966, APPENZELL with its flower frescoes, & many decorative metal inn signs, was our local town, & the cog railway down & up, fun to use. Later, friends in the Austrian Montafon Valley met us in the 1st new Gaschurn village Hotel. Delightful. Have developments here, now reduced the charm, we wonder?

GAIS
HOTEL KRONE

"IN GASCHURN"
A TINY WHITE CHURCH PERCHED ON A LITTLE GREEN HILL, RIVER SWIRLING ROUND ITS FOOT, SNOWY PEAKS TOWERING ABOVE.

June 1972, we gave ourselves such a luxury touring holiday;- DOLOMITES.

[LAMMIN. "MOUNTAIN HOTELS, ALPINE FLOWERS"] well deserved, we said, after our thrifty tent & picnic self drive holiday travels.

A new experience for us to be fed & led for once, giving all our attention to sights & scenery, tho' nothing can of course transcend the joy & challenge of independent travel.

Alpine flowers at their beautiful best, the choicest 1st Class hotels. Where could one find better? Each one of distinct character, individual in every best way. EACH ONE HAD TO BE DRAWN, INSIDE AND OUT.

WE VISITED BOLZANO, ORTISEI, GARDENA VALLEY, LAKE GARDA, RIVA, GARDONE, SIRMIONE, BRESCIA, PONTRESINA, ST.MORITZ, DAVOS, KLOSTERS, ZURICH.

The Dolomites; how captivating they are; kings in the mighty mountainscape of snowy peaks.

We two agreed the most engaging village to be ORTISEI, & thither we happily returned in 1976.

Knowing the ropes & the 3 ski lifts & buses, we felt at home & gave ourselves an indulgent walking & gloating holiday.

Then Kathleen & Kurt E. invited us to stay in their Hotel in Merano, to enjoy their menues, see their Alps, & introduce us to their Alpine Hut. Our cup was overflowing.

· 3 ST BERNARD PUPS GREETED OUR ARRIVAL, DAVOS.

HAY DRIED ON WIRES

MEADOW CORPS DE BALLET FANTASY

ANEMONE SULFUREA

CLEMATIS ALPINA

DIANTHUS

ANTLIA

PHOTOGRAPHERS IN OUR PARTY.

IN BEDROOM

Hotels a delight to be in. Bedrooms charming, every attention to detail. All foods impressing, savoury, delicious. Desserts specially ambrosial.

LITTLE BY LITTLE, STEP BY STEP

LIFT FOR 12 ... STANDING UP! GOING UP! [BRIGHT YELLOW MAILBOX! POSTS]

SESSELIFT

our altitude changed from breeches, boots, snowy ski lifts, to the sun hats, dresses, & boat trips of warm Gardone

Llonja

PASTA
IN A SHOP WINDOW
MOULDED IN
MANY & VARIOUS
SHAPES

ANGEL
SEEN THRO' APERTURE
ON UPWARD CLIMB

THE ROOF OF MILAN CATHEDRAL
a thrilling oasis of soaring pinnacles.
We also visited; The Brera, Leonardo's 'Last Supper',
the Poldi Pezzoli Collection, S. Ambrogio, and
tasted our first ice cream Gateau in the Parco.

LIZARD-SPOTTING at MASER

Renzo & Amelia advised:- On no account
fail to visit Sicily. Accordingly in due
course we filled 3 weeks there with delight.
Unfortunately no pages left for a record here.
Responding, we recommended; "When next you
Visit Britain, see the W. Highlands & Glasgow."
And thither we went together.

& many
darting
at Euryalus

☆ ⬦ ☆

PEDAVENA 1953
RAIN IN ITALY

IN 70 YRS OF CYCLING
I'VE NEVER DONE THIS

P.S. VERONA 1976. FOR ONE NIGHT ONLY; SHAME!
We rose at 5.0 a.m to walk the empty streets
& squares, & to savour the ancient &
historical perspectives in this loop of the
the Adige, without let or hindrance.

GLASGOW

St. Mungo's Cathedral, dedicated 1136 completed C13, the only survivor of the South Scotland Cathedrals, though despoiled of its carved enrichments has the basic elegance of bare bones, a sturdy authority. Seen from above the Molendinar valley, between hillside trees, its slender grace & lofty dignity have a singular appeal, though coal black with the grime of years.

Within, it is distinguished by the rich moulding & detail of piers & bosses, & by the stairs leading from the crossing [recall Canterbury] up to the quire & Upper Church, & down to the vaulted Laigh or Lower Church. [recall Assisi]
In this pillared crypt lies the tomb of St Mungo founder of Glasgow d.612

The mystery of dimness struck me, entranced as I was by the pattern of arcading & shadows across the wide Laigh floor.

"With antique pillars massy proof And storied windows richly dight Casting a dim religious light." J.M.

A most compact cathedral with shallow transepts & 4, not 5 or 7 lancet lights, E·end

PULPITUM
THE CARVING UPON THIS
STONE SCREEN IS SAID TO REPRESENT:-
7 DEADLY SINS ABOVE BLIND ARCADE,
5, & 6, APOSTLES AT SIDES, BELOW

ON THE NECROPOLIS THE POETS GAVE ME:-
"Can storied urn or animated bust..... " T. Gray
"Lives of great men all remind us...... " H.W. Longfellow
"On thee shall press no ponderous tomb ..." Lord Byron

THE SURPRISING NECROPOLIS HILL
NECROPOLIS SEEN BEYOND CATHEDRAL SPIRE FROM CATHEDRAL SQ.
DO VISIT PROVANDS LORDSHIP, OLD HOUSE CLOSE BY.

Our Italian friends the Cantagallis [who had stated that Glasgow was now their oyster] were most impressed with the refinement of the Cathedral. We then climbed the unexpectedly steep & unique NECROPOLIS, [cemetery of Victorian & other magnates] a 'pincushion' of needling pinnacles & tombs; a fascinating assortment in every conceivable period style of small or large memorials. That of John Knox reigns supreme with very telling inscriptions. Other epitaphs brought to mind Greyfriars Churchyard in Edinburgh.

A pause en route showed the black Cathedral spire among leafy trees. Breath regained, we were rewarded by a clear view of Ben Lomond from the top.

PAINTED
STONE SLAB

CARVED LINTELS OF CHAPTER HSE DOORWAY IN LAIGH CHURCH, MUCH DECAYED, SHOW INTERLACED FOLIAGE WREATHING VARIOUS FIGURES, CHRIST, A BISHOP A PRIEST & SO ON.

OLD GLASGOW
WHICH LIES TO THE S.E. OF GEORGE SQ.

PROVAND'S LORDSHIP.
CATHEDRAL SQ.
OLDEST HOUSE
IN GLASGOW 1471

SLENDER
SPIRE
BARONY
CHURCH

WE
MET
MOST
HELPFUL
& KEEN
GLASWEGIAN
HERE IN
CATH. SQ.

MERCAT
CROSS
replica
1929

7 STOREY
CROWNED
TOLBOOTH
STEEPLE

TRON
STEEPLE
OF ST MARY'S
CHURCH
SURVIVING
RELIC.

4 PILED
TOWERS
OF OLD
MERCHANT
HOUSE
STEEPLE
GOLDEN GALLEON
ON SPIRE

ST ANDREW'S
PARISH CHURCH
VERY FINE PLASTER &
WOOD WORK WITHIN.

South from
Cathedral Sq
the steep slope
of High St
curves down to:-
MERCAT CROSS &
TOLBOOTH TOWER.

TRON STEEPLE
straddles the
pavement at
Trongait;

MERCHANT'S
STEEPLE
rises in
3 stages from
Bridgegate;

ST ANDREW'S
PARISH CHURCH
lies off the
Saltmarket.

After the HIGH
COURT on the R,
is ALBERT BGE
over the Clyde.

Short diversions
off this route
show Ladywell
inner city housing
estate, City Hall
memorial plaques
& many historic
associations hereabout.

PEOPLE'S PALACE of
GLASGOW ANTIQUITIES.
on Glasgow Green

MARTIN FOUNTN

SHEER DELIGHT OF
CANOPIED ENCHANTMENT
IN THIS FILIGREE OF
IRONWORK, COMMEMORATING
THE COUNCILLOR MAGISTRATE
opposite People's Palace

TROPICAL
WINTER
GARDENS
behind P. Palace
MY TAXI DRIVER ON THE WAY HERE WAS
FULL OF INFORMATION & CIVIC PRIDE. "ALL
GLASGOW NEEDS IS AN INJECTION OF MILLIONS"

GLASGOW GREEN

[common land
once, for grazing
& bleaching, the
oldest of all the
Glasgow Parks,]

A picnic here,
imagining past
orators & agitators
& folk crowding,
then to the nearby
PEOPLE'S PALACE
Museum;
but the

WINTER
GARDENS,
closed for repair;
WE ENJOYED THE
FOUNTAIN, for
James Martin
(McFarlane Foundry;)

JAMES WATT
BOULDER;

NELSON
OBELISK;

DOULTON
FOUNTAIN;

ADAM ARCH;

TEMPLETON'S;

DAISY GREEN;
THEN TO
VICTORIA BGE,
for the 1864
Wool Clipper
"Carrick".

DOULTON FOUNTAIN

TOPPED BY
QUEEN VICTORIA
IN TERRA COTTA,
EXCLUSIVE,
NOW IN DECAY,
VERY REGRETTABLY
1888

PURSE

SAID TO HAVE BEEN SEWN
BY MARY Q. OF SCOTS WHEN
IMPRISONED IN FOTHERINGAY

BOTH OF
THESE IN

THE PEOPLE'S
PALACE

3 POOR MEN OF
OLD MERCHANT
HOUSE 1659
stone carved.

Motifs
from TEMPLETON'S
CARPET FACTORY
"Doge's Palace,"
fantastic erection
on Glasgow Green.
"To see is to believe!"

THE CITY CENTRE & THEREABOUT

CITY CHAMBERS STAIRCASE

A MEMORY SKETCH, THO' INEXACT, GIVES THE FLAVOUR

THE CITY CHAMBERS

GEORGE SQ.

ENTRANCE THE CITY HALL 1841

"Once a market" said an Officer, "now a CONCERT HALL" SCOTTISH NATIONAL ORCHESTRA etc

"In Renaissance style" we agreed surveying this prestige edifice with its confident imposing grey facade against silvery clouds as it faced the spacious square which flaunted breezy buntings, jolly flower beds, a dozen statues, & Sir Walter Scott on his tall column.

In we went to be still more impressed by the grand & substantial magnificence of the interior. Victorian wealth provided this opulence of loggia, staircases, Banqueting Hall, in Italian marbles, mosaics, faience, stained glass, murals. Most spectacular.

What of special interest hereabout? Strathclyde University, [with COLLINS EXHIBITION HALL & central campus sculpture] Stirling's Library; Hutcheson's Hospital; Courthouses; Trades Hse; Sheriff Crt; City Hall; St David's [Ramshorn] Church; Pedestrian precincts; & towards the Clyde Walkway industrial buildings & warehouses of note & substance.

ST GEORGE'S TRON CHURCH CLOSES VISTA FROM GEORGE STREET WEST 1807

TWO OF GLASGOW'S MANY SPIRES

STEEPLE OF HUTCHESON'S HOSPITAL 1802 →

ST ENOCH'S UNDERGROUND STN something like this, [brain blue!] bijou, red, Jacobean, a toy, a pigmy surrounded by giants. [Jolly to draw on a larger scale!]

IN GEORGE SQUARE

PRINCE ALBERT

QUEEN VICTORIA

STIRLING'S LIBRARY

WITH DUKE OF WELLINGTON BEFORE & HANDSOME COFFERD CEILING WITHIN

A sunny day sees the many seats of George Sq gratefully enjoyed & pigeons eagerly friendly. I trained my binoculars on Sir Walter Scott & the gilded galleon in full sail topping the globe above Merchants' House [between bites of juicy nectarine.] "Yes," said our seat companion, "I also gaze up at the ship when my husband rides the high seas."

THE MUSEUM & ART GALLERY in Kelvingrove Park gives me many a day of pleasure with its rich collections.

KELVINGROVE PARK

is a delightful hilly amenity in the W of the city threaded by the River Kelvin, which in its winding course, separates the University to the N from the Art Gallery to the S.

UNIVERSITY of GLASGOW 1451; Founded GILMOREHILL dominates the Park. Here is BUTE HALL above vaulted underpass HUNTERIAN MUSEUM & ART GALLERY

IN THE KELVINGROVE ART GALLERY,

The Early Flemish Paintings [Memlinc] absorbed me:— Sparrow, hand clasped; Bed Hangings; Three cornered chair; a hand in the Fig tree etc.

SUSPENDED FROM HIS FINGER IS THE TASSELLED CORD OF CARDINAL'S SCARLET HAT

FROM NATIVITY 1450

'WINDOW SHUTTER'

How very much the contours of a city affect its appeal. Heights & dips challenge & excite the eye as well as the legs. Glasgow has its steep Necropolis to the E, and heights of The Park to the West, then many a sloping street between to give variety to its perspectives.

The bridges, & tree clad valley of the Kelvin are a bonus, also the White Cart Water of Pollok House Gdn, Linn Park, & the waterfall of Rouken Glen. Glasgow can proudly boast over 70 public Parks

IN THE HUNTERIAN ART GALLERY,

I scrutinised the lively McNeil Whistler drawings noticing the little 'butterfly' signatures & esteemed the august & sombre dignity of his paintings

1879

LORD ROBERTS at high view point, & many other memorials in PARK GARDENS. [cheese, date, nut picnic here]

KELVIN HALL across road from the Art Gallery a red sandstone building houses a seated arena, exhibition hall, cafe, restaurant etc: an entertainment centre for indoor sports, concerts, conferences, circus, etc

ELDERLY TWINS AT STUDY

DOME OF MITCHELL LIBRARY a spacious, elegant, calm retreat; & comprehensive; with over a million books. I read voraciously & mused here. On no account to be missed.

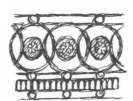

Glasgow's well known ironwork is all over the world, & too little of it remains in Glasgow.

BOTANIC GARDENS

OTHER GARDENS & IRON WORK

THE KIBBLE PALACE
LARGE DOME

What a curious name, "Kibble Palace." What can one expect to find? For me it was a tour de force in ironwork & glass, indeed a palace. Thank you warmly Mr Kibble.

The Botanic Gardens founded 1817 in Sauchiehall St moved here in 1841. The many warm greenhouses show wide varieties of orchids & so on.

[A cosy pitch for drawing]

The Kibble Palace of tree ferns etc a most alluring winter garden was brought from Coulport [Loch Long] & established here in 1873.

[Recall the tropics here!]

Approaching from the main gate I gasped, arrested by the sight of these glass houses with their fairy tale look. Once inside the main dome, I tried a sketch, the subject so simple yet so defeating; albeit the pleasantest occupation trying to sort out these confusing ellipses above the rioting green fronds & white statues.

LAMP BRACKET GORDON ST.

CATHEDRAL STANDARD LAMP

TWO WROUGHT IRON WEATHER VANE EMBLEMS BY CHARLES RENNIE MACKINTOSH

POLLOK HOUSE GARDEN VASE

LAMP STANDARD 'PEOPLES' PALACE

A twisty path leads from Kibble Palace, by many step flights down the steep wooded hillside to a footbridge across the River KELVIN

The Tree Stumps of FOSSIL GROVE, astonishingly 230 million years old, a unique world famous sight, are housed near the hilly rock garden of VICTORIA PARK

The arbours, terraces, lawns, glades, flower gardens, river, & woodland walks of POLLOK HOUSE, 1752, [by William Adam] & its fine collections on display within, should not be missed.

WHITE CART WATER

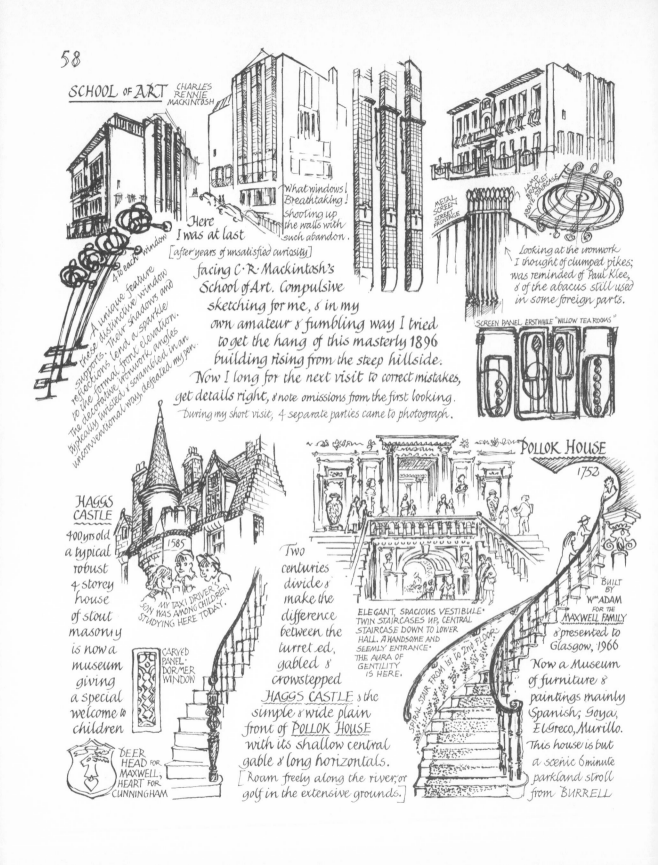

58

SCHOOL of ART

CHARLES RENNIE MACKINTOSH

What windows! Breathtaking! shooting up the walls with such abandon.

Here I was at last

[after years of unsatisfied curiosity]

facing C·R· Mackintosh's School of Art. Compulsive sketching for me, & in my own amateur & fumbling way I tried to get the hang of this masterly 1896 building rising from the steep hillside. Now I long for the next visit to correct mistakes, get details right, & note omissions from the first looking.
During my short visit, 4 separate parties came to photograph.

4 to each window

A unique feature these distinctive window supports. Their shadows and reflections lend a sparkle to the formal front elevation. The decorative ironwork angles typically twisted & scrambled in an unconventional way, defeated my pen.

METAL SCREEN STREET FRONTAGE

LAMP BRACKET ABOVE STAIRCASE

Looking at the ironwork I thought of clumped pikes; was reminded of Paul Klee, & of the abacus still used in some foreign parts.

SCREEN PANEL, ERSTWHILE "WILLOW TEA ROOMS"

HAGGS CASTLE

400 yrs old a typical robust 4 storey house of stout masonry is now a museum giving a special welcome to children

1585

MY TAXI DRIVER'S SON WAS AMONG CHILDREN STUDYING HERE TODAY.

CARVED PANEL· DORMER WINDOW

DEER HEAD FOR MAXWELL, HEART FOR CUNNINGHAM

Two centuries divide & make the difference between the turreted, gabled & crowstepped HAGGS CASTLE & the simple & wide plain front of POLLOK HOUSE with its shallow central gable & long horizontals.
[Roam freely along the river, or golf in the extensive grounds.]

ELEGANT, SPACIOUS VESTIBULE· TWIN STAIRCASES UP, CENTRAL STAIRCASE DOWN TO LOWER HALL. A HANDSOME AND SEEMLY ENTRANCE· THE AURA OF GENTILITY IS HERE.

POLLOK HOUSE

1752

BUILT BY Wm ADAM FOR THE MAXWELL FAMILY

SPIRAL STAIR FROM 1st to 2nd FLOOR

& presented to Glasgow, 1966

Now a Museum of furniture & paintings mainly Spanish; Goya, El Greco, Murillo. This house is but a scenic 6 minute parkland stroll from BURRELL

THE BURRELL COLLECTION

A PRELIMINARY TASTE · 4 SPELL BINDING HOURS WITH SIR WILLIAM'S TREASURES.

ENGLISH · NOAH'S ARK · CARVED OAK

TINY STAMP SEALS & CARVED PENDANTS ARE HERE FROM... B.C

Frequent chairs invite contemplation of the building itself, so cleverly designed to house the wide diversity of treasures, from the smallest & lightest, to the largest & heaviest.

C15 MISERICORD, WHICH AS A TIP UP SEAT WAS MEANT TO BE FELT RATHER THAN SEEN DURING LITURGY, IS HERE DISPLAYED ON EYE LEVEL FOR OUR DELECTATION

DETAIL FROM BRUSSELS LACE PANEL

STAINED GLASS

DEACON SAINT · BISHOP SAINT 1330 GERMAN

COLLECTIONS OF STAINED GLASS SPLENDIDLY DISPLAYED.

WHAT CRISP REFINED DRAWING IS EVIDENT C14

1330 ST MARY OF EGYPT

FRENCH VIRGIN & CHILD

An artist stands on a friend's back to inscribe a pillar

BY HOKUSAI 1820

From the mezzanine floor above, [closed 12·0–2·0] one can look down to objects displayed in transparent cases on the ground floor.

1600 EARTENWARE BOTTLE

PORCELAIN TEAPOT C18

& other objets d'art, & furniture to be seen in POLLOK HOUSE, 6 mins walk

THE PROPHET JEREMIAH FRENCH 1140–45

Bare bones, with nuts & bolts evident, seem very appropriate here

Apologies to architect & builder for these untailored sketches

Île de France

1325–50

C15 GERMAN 2 WORKING FIGURES MAN & WOMAN, SET IN SHIELDS. [STAINED GLASS.]

What an avid collector he was! Even samplers are here. AND WHAT OF THE BUILDING?

3 FIGURES FROM ALTAR FRONTAL WOVEN TAPESTRY 5TH GERMAN 1471–80

For me it is a purpose built museum of the highest order, considerate & complimentary to all the artifacts displayed, marrying the works of nature with those of man, as the bright October sun gilds the trees without, & plays through the glass walls weaving floor patterns within.

Glaswegians everywhere are known to be deeply
affectionate toward their city. Searching it out
we noticed this particularly when finding
our way to the Transport Museum,
which visit greatly delighted both R & E.

ONE OF
MY TAXI
DRIVERS

IN THE BARROWS

ON THE NO 12 BUS

IN THE TRANSPORT MUSEUM

ON THE TRAM

SISTER & BROTHER

ON THE WALKWAY

ON GLASGOW GREEN

IN THE PEOPLES PALACE

IN THE SUBWAY

THE PADDLE STEAMER, MEG MERRILEES 1866

RUGS PILLOWS L·M·S

MATCHES ASH TRAY

4"x4"

PENNY FARTHING BONESHAKER 1870
& TWO REMINDERS OF "ONCE UPON A TIME" ON THE L·M·S·

8 year olds at work in the Transport Museum
eager, alert & busy. Oh, that precious sense of wonder!

1864
S.V. CARRICK
NOW H·Q· R·N·V·R·
TOO COLD & WINDY
FOR MORE THAN A
RUDIMENTARY SKETCH

For Renzo & Emilia,
I filled a note book with little
memento sketches; rapid ones,
for friends must not be kept
waiting. "Next visit," they
agreed, "we must sail
down the Clyde."

SUSPENSION
FOOT BRIDGE
CROSSING THE CLYDE
ON TO GLASGOW GREEN

THE BARROWS, ALFRESCO MARKET'
WIND TODAY. BARGAINS, ' CROWDS AS EVER, & SALESMEN
WITH STRINGS OF PATTER & SPRINKLINGS OF CHEERFUL GAGS

"LET GLASGOW FLOURISH"
IS THE CITY'S MOTTO.

3 NORTHERN CAPITALS

STOCKHOLM, HELSINKI, COPENHAGEN

✩ ✩ ✩ ✩ ✩

Astrid Ekblom, during her visit to London 1957,
invited us to use her Stockholm Flat in the summer,
while she retreated to her island cottage.

OUR PLANTS
CRANESBILL
HAREBELL
VERONICA

FAMILIAR WILD LIFE

SLENDER MASTS;
DENIZENS OF THE AIR. [THIS MEMORY SKETCH IS MERELY A TOKEN.]

EXUBERANT   JOYFUL

RAINBOWS &
BALLET SCULPTURE

The terraced gardens of Carl Milles' House, Stockholm,
graced with fountains & 'air borne' bronzes, were a special delight.

22·7·57 TILBURY 530 P.M. Board SS BRITANNIA for GOTHENBURG.
Of North Sea crossings surely this was the very stormiest.
Meals went untouched. We 300, vowed, 'NEVER AGAIN!'
24·7·57 GOTHENBURG 830 A.M. The Stockholm train journey was a
welcome antidote. The Flat 10 mins from the City Centre.

The following drawings, much reduced, are taken from my Nordic Sketch Bk
1957 was the year of the FLOMASTER Felt Pen. Mine, [erratic,] never Mastered its Flo!

SWEDEN'S CAPITAL

STOCKHOLM
VENICE OF THE NORTH

PICNIC NEAR SKURU.

TOP KNOTS STADHUSET

TOP KNOTS OF RIDDARHOLM CH.
WESTMINSTER ABBEY OF STOCKHOLM

RIDDARHOLM CHURCH LACY SPIRE

TRAINING SHIP NOW YOUTH HOSTEL MOORED, SHEPPSHOLMEN

MUSHROOM SHELTER IN THE STUREPLAN. WAIT HERE FOR 10

BOAT TRIPS TO ISLANDS OF SALTSJON BEYOND DJURGARDEN, SKURU, AGA...

VIKING BROOCHES

A MOORING BETWEEN OPERA & PARLIAMT

KINGSTRADGATEN, SVEAGATEN, RUNEBERGSGATEN, TEGNERGATEN, ALSO GAVE US PLEASANT SEATS IN FREQUENT RETREATS

100 öre = 1 Krone, 14 Krone = £1

AN ODENGATEN MEMORY
ALSO VISITED KLARASTRAND, & KONSERTHUSET MARKETS

3 TOP 8
STOREYS OF 8 STOREY HOUSE!
KORNHAMNSTAG OPPOSITE MARKET

Dear A, **STOCKHOLM 18 Aug '57**

We've returned to your flat [after dissipating our last Finnish marks on our round trip, Abo, Naantali, Helsinki,] as natives coming home; & now back again to Swedish krona, have shopped locally & filled the fridge to bursting. The trusty No 7 tram deposited us at yr front door where letters for both were lying on the mat.

Since your departure we've made acquaintance with neighbours, their homes, their dogs; have been whisked off to Sigtuna [St Olaf's 1050, "military" churches, Runic stones & splendid dinner at the Green Dragon] then swept across open country to gold tinted bogs of UPPSALA for coffee with student, & spanked round the town, University, Cathedral [SWEDENBORG], then a detour for party with friends; making an exciting day's driving, with peeps into Swedish life. Apart from the lack of hedges, walls, the countryside seems familiar to us, & the food while distinctive is happily not exotic. We much enjoy the deer meat, herrings, smorgasbord, buns.

Drottingholm Palace [the Versailles of Stockholm] & its C18 Theatre, which reminded us of the Bristol Royal, are alone worth our journey to Stockholm, we think.

Stockholm is a lovely city, & spruce port, sparkling among its many waters, islands, bridges, & graced by its well dressed, tall, golden girls. We've enjoyed Carl Milles' Garden, [thrilling, specially to me as a former sculptor] & Skansen of course, with all its pleasures. Djurgarden & Waldemarsudde gave us a sunny day & boat trips have made us known to the Quay boys. We've taken a picnic daily tho' Swedes appear not to eat alfresco.

I've haunted exclusive Museums while M. has been housewife, we've ferreted out markets between skyfalls, visited the Royal Palace Riddarholm, & the Stadthuset, & have never once envied the tourists from the "Arcadia," anchored in midstream, & their cosseted lives! We very probably consumed more 'rasps' & 'straws' than they!

Schnapps, milk, & & Knäckebröd.

ONE THINKS OF ALFRED NOBEL, STRINDBERG, SWEDENBORG, LINNAEUS, AXELMUNTHE.....

ZAND OF TIMBER, LAKES, & SAUNA.

FINLAND

14½ HRS SAIL

3·8·57· 6·0 P.M· 600+ FOLK. Board S.S. WELLAMO for TURKU. Boat, thick with passengers. Girl Guides returning from Jamboree in Britain, & wearing charms for a safe passage. We nosed our way between countless islands of the

archipelago, wondering should we spot Astrid's cottage! Folk were huddled together with their luggage just as on our Western Isles Ferries for the night crossing. We slept like the dead in our cosy cabin. Meals were heralded, not by gong, but by tuneful Glockenspiel.

TURKU 830 A.M· 4·8·57

Hotel impeccable. Mrs Zindmann [University] gave warm welcome. With tram, bus, taxi at hand, visited Ⓡ Cathedral, Castle, Craft Centre, Observatory, University, Museum, River. VERY FULL DAYS!

COTTAGE MUSEUM CRAFTSMEN AT WORK:- GOLDSMITH, POTTER, PAINTER, COBBLER, PRINTER, BLOCK MAKER, BOOK BINDER, SCULPTOR, WEAVER.

CASTLE FORT now being repaired of damage from World War II.

TURKU HAS ICE FREE PORT. WAS ONCE CAPITAL CITY

FGW MOTIFS EMBROIDERY

NANTAALI, INLETS, LITTLE BATHING BAYS, 'PORPOISE' ROCKS, BOATS, ISLANDS   MEDICAL BATHS

We relaxed in Naantali, Spa Town 8 mls off; low villas of wood, Spa Rooms built on piles above sea, great smooth granite rocks curving down into the sea. Diving, sun bathing.

A GOOD THING WE BOOKED OUR SEATS ON THE HELSINKI TRAIN, 3½ hrs. IT WAS CRAMMED! WE SHARED OUR MARKET RASPS WITH GERMAN YOUTH [SPORTS GROUP] & GAVE THEM OUR SAUNA TWIGS.

HELSINKI CAPITAL CITY

MASSIVE BULK OF RUSSIAN ORTHODOX CHURCH

RUGS LAUNDERED

ABOVE THE SEA

CATHEDRAL DOMES & PRESIDENT'S PALACE, ABOVE THE SPARKLING MARKET, GAY AWNINGS, BOBBING BOATS, FLOWERS, WEAVING ETC.

PASSENGERS AT BREAKFAST

A FINE CITY. NO SLUMS. REMEMBER GRANITE FACADES OF RLY STN, MUSEUMS WITH LAPLAND CULTURE

THE CLIMB UP OBSERVATORY HILL FOR VIEWS, WAS WORTH OUR EFFORT.

TWIN BERTHS IN A CHARMING CABIN

Hotel in Esplanade, tree lined. Smart shops. Harbour market most alluring, buying from peasants in their boats opposite the stretch of dignified Renaissance Bdgs, Pres. Palace & Stadthuset.
I'll always remember the turquoise domes of the Cathedral, presiding at the top of the sloping Square with University Bdgs forming a fine architectural unit, then the wide flight of stone steps leading down to Senate Square below.
In Brunnsparken, on the coast, our joy of sunlit evenings, laughing women scrubbed away at their rugs on floating jetties. Museums much enjoyed.
A steady return sail, very restful, to Stockholm. Will post this after Copenhagen jaunt.

64

DENMARK'S CAPITAL
25·8·'57 COPENHAGEN. ZEALAND.

CHRISTIANSBORG CANAL NEAR STROGET.

Looking across to busy shipyards from our picnic spot in Garden by yachting harbour.

HANS ANDERSON'S LITTLE MERMAID

STOCKHOLM — COPENHAGEN
12 HRS. 3 trains, 1 ferry.

Our stay here was far
too short; so much to
see & enjoy around & about:-

Ships & canals among city streets;
Fish quays; fruit markets, [4 fruit trees
to every Dane, they say], red coated postmen;
Meal rituals; fish dinners; kraftor,
[crayfish] smoked eel, plaice, smörrebröd;
schnapps.
Friendliness of folk;

CITY OF BIKES & BOATS & CANDLES

Quay side colour; Tivoli Gardens,
with high spirits, lights, balloons, fun;
Christiansborg Palace;
elaborate green copper spires;
Amalienborg Palace,
in its Octagonal Square;
the Latin Quarter;
red roofs, old houses & streets, cellars;
Stroget shops, [our candles, my 1st MOBILE]
Museums; pipe, cigar smoking women;
Bathing tents like teepees;
the spiral slope of brick paving
up the Round Tower.

FRAG MENTS OF ONE OF DENMARK'S MANY CHURCH WALL PAINTGS AT MAALOV CHURCH (3
BY TRAIN & TAXI

BEACH TENTS

GOLDEN SPIRAL STAIRWAY, OUR SAVIOUR'S CH, CHRISTIANSHAVN

CHRISTIANSBORG PALACE SPIRE, WITH BALLS & CROWNS

ROYAL EXCHANGE STEEPLE, 4 SPIRALLING DRAGON TAILS

A SMALL SELECTION OF MANY OF THE DISTINCTIVE STEEPLES

MAARSTRAND ISLAND SWEDEN.
MAARSTRAND
TRAM FERRY
Local women, circumspect in black costumes & black straw hats

On both journeys, we enjoyed glimpses:- ELSINORE
& MALMO; later from GOTHENBURG
we visited MAARSTAND ISLAND, Bohuslan,
for sun & sea nude bathing.

ONE OF MALMO'S OPEN SPACES

ON SUN DECK OF FERRY

GAMMELTORV SQUARE STROGET

FULL TRAIN MALMO TO GOTHENBURG

We have you, Astrid,
to thank for prompting
these happy glimpses
of 3 Northern Capitals
& their surroundings.
Come to Britain again soon.
Best wishes to you, MMB & DAG.

DOCK AREA ALIVE WITH SHIPS

SS PATRICIA GOTHENBURG TO LONDON

ON ONE OF HER LATER ARRIVALS HERE, ASTRID WAS KEEN TO VISIT THE NORTHERN CITY OF ABERDEEN.

A LOOK AT THE CITY OF ABERDEEN

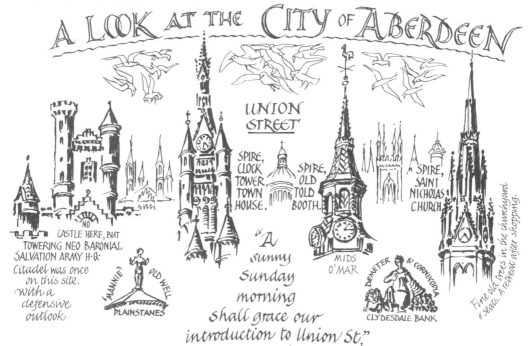

UNION STREET

SPIRE, CLOCK TOWER, TOWN HOUSE.

SPIRE, OLD TOLD BOOTH.

SPIRE, SAINT NICHOLAS CHURCH.

NO CASTLE HERE, BUT TOWERING NEO BARONIAL SALVATION ARMY H.Q. Citadel was once on this site. with a defensive outlook.

'MANNIE', OLD WELL PLAINSTANES

MIDS O'MAR

DEMETER & CORNUCOPIA CLYDESDALE BANK

Fine old trees in the churchyard 8 seats. A retreat after shopping.

"A sunny Sunday morning shall grace our introduction to Union St,"

we declared, 8 walked the granite highway along to Castle Gate savouring on the way its plain dignity. Granite sparkling, seagulls screaming, turreted clock towers 8 spires climbing the sky, fine old mercat cross centrally placed, I found this a most attractive square to draw 8 linger in. [Go thro' Lodge Walk arched pend to view the corbelled bartizans of the old Tolbooth Tower.]

Roadside harlequin rosebeds in plenty scent the salty air 'BRITAIN IN BLOOM AWARD

GATE CREST

KING EDWARD VII'S ROSTRUM,

"It was roses, roses all the way." R.B.

at west end of UNION BRIDGE, gives south facing perches for many folk. Looking down, we realised Aberdeen City boasts two levels. Below, Union Gardens, the road, the rail, make Bridge Sts union, into fly-overs. 14 sculptured leopards on the bridge parapet are called 'Kelly's Cats' after the designer. St Nicholas' columned screen 8 trees make a desirable interlude in this main street, north side. "Aberdeen – that's a city to be born in" it is acclaimed.

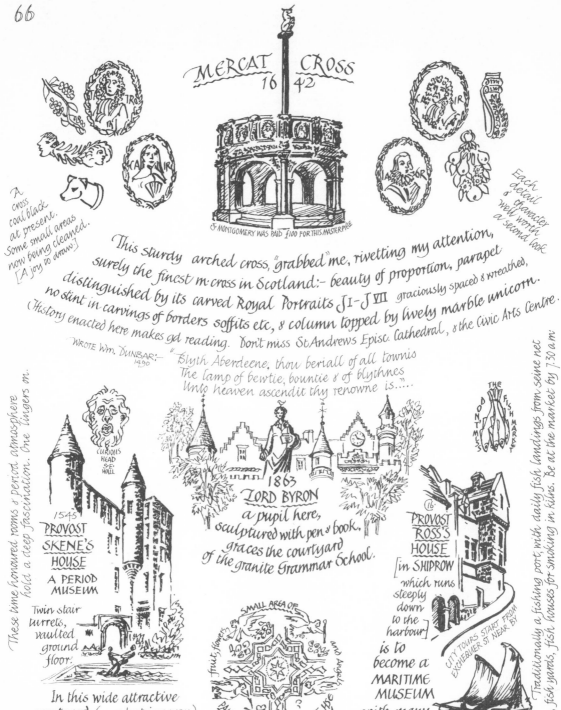

MERCAT CROSS
16 42

J. MONTGOMERY WAS PAID £100 FOR THIS MASTERPIECE

A cross coal black at present. Some small areas now being cleaned. [A joy to draw.]

Each detail & character well worth a second look

This sturdy arched cross, "grabbed" me, rivetting my attention, surely the finest m. cross in Scotland:- beauty of proportion, parapet distinguished by its carved Royal Portraits JI-J VII graciously spaced & wreathed, no stint in carvings of borders soffits etc, & column topped by lively marble unicorn. History enacted here makes gd reading. Don't miss St Andrews Episc. Cathedral, & the Civic Arts Centre.

WROTE WM. DUNBAR:- 1490

"Blyth Aberdeene, thou beriall of all townis
The lamp of bewtie, bountie & of blythnes
Unto heaven ascendit thy renowne is....."

These time honoured rooms & period atmosphere hold a deep fascination. One lingers on.

CURIOUS HEAD S.E. WALL

1545
PROVOST SKENE'S HOUSE
A PERIOD MUSEUM

Twin stair turrets, vaulted ground floor.

In this wide attractive courtyard, (a pedestrian way,) we took an avocado picnic.

1863
LORD BYRON
a pupil here, sculptured with pen & book, graces the courtyard of the granite Grammar School.

SMALL AREA OF fruit, flowers and Angels
PAINTED CEILING IN P.SKENE 1850

THE FISH MARKET
DONT MISS

16.
PROVOST ROSS'S HOUSE
[in SHIPROW
which runs steeply down to the harbour]
is to become a
MARITIME MUSEUM
with many displays in 1984

CITY TOURS START FROM EXCHEQUER ST NEAR BY

Traditionally a fishing port, with daily fish landings from seine net boats, fish yards, fish houses for smoking in kilns. Be at the market by 7.30 a.m.

ART GALLERY

HIS MAJESTY'S THEATRE

DOME LIGHT

HENRY MOORE

SCULPTURES

A most exhilarating Entrance, light spacious. Very fine collections; elegant & gracious rooms for the exhibits.

Theatres should delight, immediately one enters. This certainly does. Enchantment lies here. Surely this is the pride of Aberdeen, a precious possession; lovely to view & observe, a pleasure to sit in even before the music sounds & the curtain rises.

EPSTEIN'S SCULPTURE "GIRL WITH FLOWERS"

QUITE BEYOND MY POWER TO DRAW

Busy Lizzies, pansies, fuchsias etc, drape window boxes

UNION ST above, CORRECTION WYND Below, & curved retaining wall of St Nicholas churchyard, spacious with trees & set with many seats. Fine stone columned screen

SPIRAL STAIR OF TOWN HOUSE GLIMPSED FROM UNDERNEATH & LOOKING UP TO SKY LIGHT.

AN APOLOGY, THO' A MEMORY SKETCH, IN MINUTES, RIDICULOUS TO TRY A STANDING DAY IS REQUIRED. WHEN A SEATED

THE CHARTER ROOM HERE IS OF GREAT INTEREST & A FINE COLLECTION OF CIVIC PORTRAITS ALSO IN THE TOWN HOUSE.

ENTRANCE MITCHELL HALL
CEREMONIALS, CONCERTS, ITEMS, YOUTH INTERNATION·ORCHESTRAS.

MARISCHAL COLLEGE (Just a skyline flavour) Founded 1597, merged with Kings College 1860.

BEYOND MY POWERS, BUT SOMETHING LIKE THIS

I did not count the bristling pinnacles in such a sky pricking skyline or the galaxy of stiffly gleaming gilded pennons in this facade of verticals, reminding of Houses of Parliament. THE MITCHELL TOWER HOUSES PICTURE GALLERY & MUSEUM. "THAY HAIF SAID, WHAT SAY THEY: LAT YAME SAY"

HERALDIC ENTRANCE TO QUAD

OLD ABERDEEN
THE AULTON
TOWN & GOWN

ST MACHAR'S CATHEDRAL 1440

KING'S COLLEGE CHAPEL
CROWN TOWER 1634
FOUNDED 1495

A Few Jottings

Off now by bus, towards the River Don, a pleasant short ride. Saunter along the quiet byways around High St. See old stone walls, Kings College precincts, crests, coats of arms, Grant's Place, Wrights & Coopers Place & Town House. On along Chanonry to Botanic Gardens, then to St Machar's Cathedral. All this a most contemplative experience, sequestered, leisured, casting its spell of agelong earlier times.

"Neth Marischal's spire, or King's auld croon
In hodden grey or scarlet goon,
For future fechts we laid the 'foun'
In Aiberdeen awa.' "
CHARLES MURRAY

CROWN UPON CROWN

CURIOUS CURVED BUTTRESSES

As I feebly draw with marvelling veneration, I ask "HOW DID THEY DO IT?"

THE TWIN SPIRES OF THIS FORTIFIED, MACHICOLATED CATHEDRAL WITH FINE HERALDIC CEILING 1520

GATE LAMP
ST MACHAR'S CATHEDRAL

"Fair Quiet, have I found thee here," A MARVELL.

SUNDIAL

sheltered seats in this enchanting backwater of Wrights & Cooper's Place

TOWN HOUSE
neat, compact, centrally placed dividing the roadway. A student bus 20 brings you here.

An indulgent taxi lad, who cut off the meter, & escorted me with entertaining tales around the romantic Brig o' Balgownie

special pleasure, the steep walk down the cobbled street past old world cottages

TO THE BRIG O' BALGOWNIE

THE SINGLE SPAN BRIG O' BALGOWNIE 1329 ACROSS THE NARROWS OF THE RIVER DON

Generations have loved & sung this romantic & venerable brig. Its fame is world wide. Leaning on the parapet, my taxi man confessed he made his marriage proposal here.

RIVER DON

BRIG O' DON 1830.
The original benefaction ensuring upkeep of the old brig, so much increased in value, it more than met the £16,000 req. for the new bridge.

THE COAST OF ABERDEEN
FAIR CITY OF RIVERS TWAIN

GOLF   GOLF & HARE BELLS BLOWING   HAREBELLS

The view from Torry Point, [an approximate scribble:]
with the seaport city lying between Rivers Dee to S. & Don to N, gives infinite variety
of scene: 2 mls of beaches backed by sand dunes & golf course with Old Aberdeen to the
north, 3 busy harbours below the city spires; Pocra Quay, Round House, Footdee, piers, lighthouse.

Who would not spend a sunny day (wind there may well be), on Girdleness headland, delectable spot; with
binoculars scanning the docks, oil rigg supply craft, the comings
& goings of ships; picnic at hand, golf clubs at the ready, then a
sunset walk by Nigg Bay & along cliffs to the south & of course a sketch pad?

HOUSES IN FOOTDEE (FITTIE)

'Out of this world' is the
compact, secluded and
ancient fishing village,
on the point by Pocra Quay.
Two Squares, N & S; Middle Row & Pilot
Square added later. Originally these
homes were but & ben cottages. Windy? Yes!

THE ROUND HSE
H.Q. OF PILOTS.
HARBOUR
BOARD.
POCRA
QUAY.

A spectacle of
ships & cranes galore
in the harbour below
Custom Hse tower & Town House
spire. DON'T MISS THE FISH MARKET 7.0-9.0
a.m.

PACK HORSE BRIG 1694   over Ruthrieston Burn

Originally
without parapets, to ease the
passage of laden packhorses.
ANOTHER CHOICE PICNIC SPOT.

A second kindly taxi man who
took me to the Shakkin Briggie, turned
off his meter to inspect
the PACK HORSE BRIG, a new sight to him,
giving me 2 mins for a sketch

"I fain wad dook in Dee aince mair
An clatter doon the Mercat stair,
O the caller dilse an partans there!
The fish-wives mutches braw!"
CHARLES MURRAY 1864-1941.

1527   BRIG O' DEE   Coats & farms all along

Widened 1842
Seven ribbed arches,
recesses for walkers, steps
down to the grassy bank.

ABERDEEN'S MANY PARKS

I fell in love with DUTHIE PARK :– children's boating pool, & duck by the River Dee; the menagerie of animal sculptures for climbing, [a carver's joy] the hill mount of many coloured roses; the band stand a real charmer; the ironwork gates; the restaurant; & the Winter Garden, a stunning array of colour & vigorous growth in all the greenhouses, rushing stream & outsize goldfish.

VICTORIA PARK

Here I sat in the peace of the Blind Garden, listening to many notes of fountain music & sniffing the scents.

RUBISLAW PLEASURE GARDEN

an enticing & charming stretch of roadside parkland.

JOHNSTON GARDEN

a small 'secret' garden, full of surprises, pools, water fowl rustic bridges, twisting paths & arbours.

Just trip down the steps of Union Terrace for a south facing seat, [with a grape or 2.] in this sheltered sunken garden

ROSEMOUNT VIADUCT

Here see the Floral Clock, Aberdeen's Arms & 'Welcome', all arrayed in countless tiny plants packed close together.

Aberdeen has a wealth of retreats of great variety by the roadside or a short bus ride. So rest your bones, or exercise your muscles, & munch your apple. I had to miss Hazelhead, Seaton, Westburn Parks, & others.

Aberdeen has won the honour of top place, 'BRITAIN IN BLOOM' competition many times in succession.

MORNING TRAINS
FROM ABERDEEN, MADE POSSIBLE A BREAK, FOR AN
INVIGORATING WALK AT STONEHAVEN 1½ hrs

THE ALBERT INSTITUTE FORESTAIR; GRAND,
STATELY, IMPOSING.
A searing bitter wind
hastened this sketch

Dear BJP,

An illustrated note to thank you for the hint that Astrid should see St Andrews. After Stonehaven, the train from Aberdeen showed us full tide in Montrose Basin; the wide sands of lovely Lunan Bay; the Abbey of Arbroath [Inchcape Rock & Smokies!] Carnoustie's Golf links; then came that town of substance DUNDEE, sloping down to the silvery waters of Tay.

Its high spot for us was indeed THE LAW, 572'. What views all around 360°, with the 2 ml long Rail Bridge curving across the Firth, & the ruler straight Road Bridge. How perfectly situated above the town is this jolly volcanic cone of a grandstand.

THE BULGING FRIGATE
H.M.S. UNICORN
much interested me

THE "OLD STEEPLE" (IS
ST MARY'S KIRK
N.B. The Mills Observatory
is in BALGAY PARK

Did you ever sit in the Old Howff [with apple & cheese]; see the remarkable Unicorn Frigate; take an up river trip; contemplate the historic Tower (is of St Mary's; see the splendid Albert Art Galleries & Museum?? I know you'll have pondered before the Wishart Arch, E Port. Dundee has several covered shopping centres now. I admired the water curtain in the Wellgate Centre; & the children gloated on that extraordinary clock.

I SHALL VISIT DUNDEE AGAIN, BOTANIC GARDENS, ETC, & WILL WRITE AGAIN THEN,

THE HOWFF
DUNDEE'S OLD CEMETERY IN
CENTRE OF CITY, ANCIENT TOMBSTONES
UNDER WEEPING ASH TREES

& so to ST ANDREWS, a really delightful visit to this compact town of considerable antiquity. Astrid was enchanted. We agreed it has an aura quite of its own, gracious, old world, dreaming, & yet populous & busy with Royal & Ancient, Town & Gown, & Tourism. The way the 3 main streets converge easterly towards the Cathedral Precincts, makes the town plan distinctive & memorable.

A memory sketch

DUNDEE'S E·PORT, OLD COWGATE,
THE WISHART ARCH, where G·W·
is said to have preached 1544

The Pends lead to
ST ANDREWS' HARBOUR

THE PENDS
(14 PRIORY GATEHOUSE

ST ANDREWS 'W· PORT 1589
substantially restored 1843

These skeletal remains are to me, spectral, macabre, and grievous, but impressively indispensable to St Andrews' image. What distinction of beauty once was here!

ST. ANDREWS, & PERTH

Today, Sunday, gave the joyful spectacle of red gowned students walking the harbour pier, [University, F. 1412] a picturesque corner.

We wandered the streets, pends, wynds, vennels, passing old red tiled cottages with forestairs; stately Regency homes; College Quads time honoured; Queen Mary's thorn tree, & that wide spreading holm oak; St Salvator's & the Town Kirk with C16 tower; Blackfriars; the Castle on its cliffs; the Martyrs' Monument; the Step Rock, the R & A Golf Links. No visitor should miss the intimate small Museum in No 12 North St; the Crawford Art Centre; & a taste of the Lade Braes, we both think this. Our appetites are now whetted for much more of "The very ideal of a little University City" Froude

CLOCK TOWER, ST LEONARD'S SCHOOL FOR GIRLS BOARDING & DAY

IMPRESSION OF C13 CATHEDRAL REMAINS FROM SOUTH ST. THE ROUNDEL TO LEFT, THE PENDS TO RIGHT.

ST RULE'S TOWER C12 BEYOND

MY MEMORY IMPRESSION OF MEDIEVAL REMAINS ABOVE THE HARBOUR – TOO RAW FOR 'IN SITU' SKETCH NB: GOLF LINKS, R & A. TO E OF TOWN CATHEDRAL & HARBOUR TO W. OF TOWN

OLD WELL

DEAN'S CRT

From Dundee, over the Sidlaw Hills to PERTH. Yes, the city's enchantment lies in the river setting & the Inches. What miles of pleasure the lovely TAY salmon river provides in all its length. We walked its N. Inch bank as you suggested looking across to elegant terrace houses. Then the Museum. A most stylish unusual interior. The Sculpture Court arcading intrigued me, exhibits & paintings most interesting.

C15 SPIRE OF S. JOHN'S FINE KIRK RUDELY HEMMED IN BY ENCROACHING BUILDINGS

The Fair Maid's enticing spiral stair led up to a good Exhibition; the Round House [water tower] Inf. Centre, sent us up Kinnoull for a view we'd regret to have missed; the Library & long established Theatre both entertained; but S. John's Kirk was closed. Branklyn Gdns beautiful. EACH ONE OF THESE 3 CITIES MAKES A VERY GOOD CENTRE. SO EXPLORE AROUND WE MUST.

With our thanks to you & good wishes from A. E & D. A. G.

INSIDE THE MUSEUM & ART GALLERY, PERTH

1771 PERTH BRIDGE, LOOKING N, 9 ARCHES [RED SANDSTONE] OVER THE R. TAY IN SPATE TODAY

LOOKING S. FROM PERTH BGE TO THE 1960 QUEEN'S BGE

IN AUSTRIA 1937

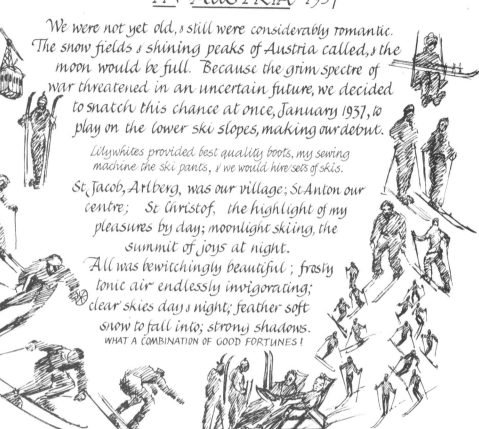

We were not yet old, & still were considerably romantic.
The snow fields & shining peaks of Austria called, & the
moon would be full. Because the grim spectre of
war threatened in an uncertain future, we decided
to snatch this chance at once, January 1937, to
play on the lower ski slopes, making our debut.

*Lilywhites provided best quality boots, my sewing
machine the ski pants, & we would hire sets of skis.*

St Jacob, Arlberg, was our village; St Anton our
centre;   St Christof, the highlight of my
pleasures by day; moonlight skiing, the
summit of joys at night.
All was bewitchingly beautiful ; frosty
tonic air endlessly invigorating;
clear skies day & night; feather soft
snow to fall into; strong shadows.
WHAT A COMBINATION OF GOOD FORTUNES !

Later on in the year 1937, though war
was still ominous, the hoarded idea
of taking a canoe down the Danube
from Passau to Vienna prevailed.
It was an opportunity not to be
missed. We would then stretch our
legs in the Fränkische Schweitz

A RAIL JOURNEY, LONDON to PASSAU, THEN:—
TO VIENNA BY CANOE FROM PASSAU 1937

We bought Thomas Cook's Railway Time Table of EUROPE,
& rattled our way by train from LONDON to PASSAU on DANUBE.
There with deft assurance we built our light canoe:—
With hope we lowered it in the fast flowing waters;
with faith we gingerly settled into it, & with great enthusiasm
we took to the paddles & eagerly practised our strokes.

6 LONG RIBS
4 CROSS STRUTS
LADDER BASE
CANVAS AND
RUBBER SKIN
Thoughts of Hiawatha

But shortly, where the swirling waters of the Inn churn into the
Danube, the wake of an untimely passing steamer intruded, facing
our tiny craft with perilous walls of
water. Great threatening waves
bore down on us in terrifying succession.
Fear gripped. "KEEP YR WITS & MEET THEM HEAD ON"
was the command from behind. I steeled myself,
fate in the balance, & feeling alone in a drowning
world, shot each one dead centre, WAVE 1 [& I was still alive]
WAVE 2, [I still breathed,] WAVES 3, 4, 5, each with
increasing confidence. The current now swept us along, the ordeal
was over, the initiation completed. We had won through.

HOKUSAI 1760-1849

THE FULL SIGNIFICANCE OF HOKUSAI'S "THE BREAKING WAVE" NOW BURST UPON ME, BRILLIANTLY REVEALED.

PASSAU, FINELY SITED ON A SPIT OF LAND BETWEEN DANUBE & INN

Old buildings line the waterfronts & streets rise steeply
to the high centre of the old
City where picturesque
houses jostle, & the
splendid Cathedral
dominates all. St Stephen's
is said to have the largest
organ in the world.

RIVER INN
RIVER DANUBE
CONFLUENCE OF THE INN, ILZ & RIVER DANUBE

St Stephen's PASSAU DOM
highly ornate
enriched barrel vault,
octagonal dome over X ing
semi ⊙ W window
Two towers on
West facade.

So, joining the party, we paddled our way down the blue Danube [often grey, sometimes rain pricked,] now idly drifting in the fast flowing stream, [approx 5 m.p.h.] now negotiating cross currents or shooting rapids [albeit of a minor nature!] parking delightfully for riverside village Inn lunches; tying up for a homely night's lodging; singing cheerily with the locals; [no T.V. of course] visiting castles, monasteries, towns, & villages bright with garden vines.

GERMAN & BRITISH FOLK SONGS EXERCISED OUR VOCAL CHORDS—

THE PADDLES EXERCISED OUR ARMS BUT WHAT IDLE LEGS!!!

Good local meals, spotless linen, embroidered lambrequins, friendly hospitable barefoot cycling peasants, enticing white field tracks, flowery paths, starry meadows.

WHAT A RIVETING SIGHT, THESE CASCADES OF COLOUR BILLOWING FROM ARCADED BALCONIES OF THE LANDHAUS, LINZ MORNING GLORY, PETUNIAS, PELARGONIUM, GERANIUM, & HOW ATTRACTIVE THE ARCHES & ARCADING OF FINE ARCHITECTURE.

THIS IS THE BAREST PRECIS, A MINIMAL INDICATION, TO PINPOINT A FEW OF THE FLAVOURS OF THIS JAUNT DOWNSTREAM SOME 300 KMS VIA ENGELHARTZEL, UNTERMÜHL, LINZ, MAUTHEUSEN, GREIN, ST·NICHOLA, YBBS, MELK, AGGSBACH, DÜRNSTEIN, KREMS, TULLN, — THEN THE LAST LAP BY TRAIN TO THE CITY OF VIENNA

GREINBURG ANOTHER ARCADED COURTYARD — 3 TIERS — TO CHARM THE EYE

CASTLE OF AGGSTEIN · HILLY VIEWS ON TO DANUBE BELOW

OUR LEGS WERE NOT IN TRAINING FOR THIS PRECIPITOUS STEEP CLIMB.

WILD CYCLAMEN AUTUMN CROCUS

EMBROIDERY OF LAMBREQUINS

MELK MONASTERY SOARING HIGH ABOVE THE WATER OF THE DANUBE

Splendid, spectacular! What impact as we rounded a bluff; a coup d'œil! this imposing snow white monastery crowning & listed high on the wooded crag, — is a majestic building on a bountiful site, stupendous proportions, simple in essence, memorable.

THE CITY OF SONG MUSIC OPERA WALTZES & GOOD CHEER

VIENNA JOTTINGS

In this "City of Music" one could not avoid noting:-

SCHUBERTRING, HÄNDELGASSE, WAGNERGASSE, BEETHOVENPLATZ, HAYDNGASSE, STRAUSS GASSE SCHUMANNGASSE, BRAHMSPLATZ, MOZARTPLATZ, ETC. Also honoured are:- SCHWEIZERGARTEN FARADAYGASSE, IBSENGASSE GOETHEGASSE & many more.

So much to see
So much to ponder on.

[Very helpful therefore to learn something of the City's great history & to study its map.]

Eyes left, eyes right,
look up, look down,
note this, draw that.
A city packed with interest:-

THE RING with its Squares, Boulevards, Avenues, Gardens Quai, & fine handsome Buildings.

THE SPLENDID STATE OPERA HOUSE, CONCERT HALLS, BURG THEATRE, MUSEUMS, GALLERIES, & fine Collections, Archives, Treasures.

ST STEPHEN'S CATHEDRAL & many fine Churches.

THE OLD TOWN, huddled houses, alleys, markets, with scents of spices, bakings.

THE HOFBURG, THE LOWER & UPPER BELVEDERE, SCHÖNBRUNN, & many other sumptuous Palaces with scintillating apartments, & THE SPANISH RIDING SCHOOL

We enjoyed Viennese cooking. Tafelspitz, Bischosbrok. Schnitzel, Sachertorte, Linzertort, Strudel, Heurigen [new wine] & Beisel, Coffee houses & cellars, Mokka, Einspanner & THE MARKETS.

THE GLORJETTE OF SCHÖNBRUNN, CROWNS MOST INVITINGLY THE WIDE GREEN HILL WHICH RISES FROM THE PALACE TERRACES.

IN SCHÖNBRUNN ONE OF A SERIES OF ORNATE PAINTED & GILT FRAMED WALL PANELS LINING THE LOFTY MILLION ROOM 1760.
*
EACH ODD SHAPED PAINTING, DELICATELY COLOURED SHOWS CONTEMPORARY LEISURE PASTIMES.

WHAT CURLICUES! WHIMSICAL! CAPRICIOUS! ECCENTRIC! BAROQUE! ROCOCO!

6 SIDED CROWNED LAMP PILLAR MOUNTED IN THE PARK SCHÖNBRUNN To draw one minor work, can epitomise for me a whole local atmosphere.

LAMP IN COURTYARD OF HOUSE WHERE SCHUBERT WAS BORN 1797

FIR BUNCHED ON POLE SIGNIFIES NEW SEASON'S WINE - But we say:- "Good wine needs no bush"!

TOP KNOT; IRON WORK GATE TO ORANGERY 1714, OF LOWER BELVEDERE. I much like the fringe of wispy curlicues, one feels deep gratitude for these 'minor' works of art

THE GRACEFUL LACELIKE HEXAGONAL TOWER OF ST. MARIA AM GESTADE This spire was a joyful focal point for me. Such a trivial sketch pays small tribute to this lofty gem.

I HAD TO NOTE - ENCAPSULATE - THIS ASTONISHING NEO GOTHIC RATHAUS WHOSE RICH FACADE LEFT ME GASPING.

UPPER BELVEDERE - LIVELY MAIN ENTRANCE. HORSE SCULPTOR UNKNOWN 1730 I much like making friends with sculptured steeds!

PRINCE EUGENE COURTYARD NEW HOFBURG.

APOSTLE 1290 LAST JUDGEMENT W. FACADE ST STEPHEN

CARVED WALL IMAGE - STONE MASON & HAMMER

ST. STEPHEN'S CATHEDRAL THE STEEPLY PITCHED ROOF IS LOZENGE PATTERNED WITH COLOURED GLAZED TILES, YELLOW BLACK & THE S.W. ROOF SHOWS THE DOUBLE HEADED HAPSBURG EAGLE TWICE TWICE OVER!! THE SPIRE, AN ACHIEVEMENT OF SINGULAR BEAUTY, IS THE PRIDE OF THE CATHEDRAL.

WE HUMMED MELODIES, THEMES, TUNES, SCHUBERT'S SONGS, SNATCHES, WE DANCED; WALTZED, PARTICULARLY OF COURSE TO STRAUSS. I HAD THE GOOD FORTUNE TO MEET PROF CIZEK IN HIS STUDIO; A PIONEER HE WAS, LEADING THE WAY TO FREEDOM OF EXPRESSION FOR CHILDREN IN THEIR ART.

Filled with the sights of Vienna & still primed with our lyrical skimming of the Danube waters, we returned to PASSAU back upstream in the Pleasure Steamer relaxing in leisured contemplation, glimpsing from its higher viewpoint the towns & villages we'd visited when canoeing, & blessing the slow downstream hours of close contact with silvery waters.

'ZUM GREIFEN' SIGN, DINKELSBÜHL BUT WHAT A PLETHORA OF BEWILDERING TWISTS IN ITS ORNAMENTAL SUPPORT! TOO FUSSY. I GAVE UP!

BAVARIA

Dear Homefolk,   Nuremberg, 20·8·1937

We've decided to extend our travels hereabout. It might possibly be our last chance, for [perish the thought] there is apprehension & foreboding. War could be upon us before long. Is it rumbling? We sense rumours in these parts, & see ominous signs, but dread such a harrowing prospect. IT MUST NOT —
—CANNOT HAPPEN• WAR WOULD PARALYSE COMMUNICATIONS, DEAL DEATH & DESTRUCTION AND SEAL US INEVITABLY IN OUR ISLAND. FOR HOW LONG? So we'll explore further while the going is good — 'no time like the right time.'......⟩

GASTHOF INN SIGN ROTHENBURG

Snatches of Wagner sang in my mind as I drew

We desired terra firma, needing to stretch our canoe legs across new countrysides. The narrow valleys among the dolomitic hills of FRANCONIA [BAVARIA] with their cliffs & castles & caves, gave good walking; local trains & buses gave lively journeying; Youth Hostels provided various & interesting companionship; & rivers gave delightful soft water bathing, [with bonus of blue dragon flies darting among water lilies] so invigorating during long treks in this fine walking country. We ate rye bread, black bread, gingerbread, sauerkraut ochsenmaulsalat, bralwürstel, pumpernickel, etc drank beers & local dry white wines & apfelsaft etc

TOWERS IN CLOSE SUCCESSION ALONG THE WALLS OF DINKELSBÜHL

TWO GATE TOWERS & GABLES, ROTHENBURG

The towers, turrets, bastions of the gated walls of medieval Rothenburg, Dinkelsbühl, Norlingen; the steep pitched gabled roofs; [grain stored in them] picturesque colourful house fronts, gay with window boxes; town markets; each took us back into the romantic past.

THE FAIRY TALE ASPECT OF THESE WELL KEPT WALLED MEDIEVAL [RIVER] TOWNS PROVIDES A FEAST OF INTEREST AT EVERY TURN; MARKETS, WELLS, FOUNTAINS, BRIDGES, BUTTRESSED WALLS, TOWERS OF MANY DESIGNS, HANDSOME INN SIGNS, CHARMING HOUSES, SQUARES, TRADITIONAL CUSTOMS & COSTUMES.

A's command of fluent German made all transactions smooth & easy. He was a guide whose companionship "made the miles seem too short, & the steepest braes like level paths"
                    RATCLIFFE BARNETT

WE HAD TO OMIT BAYREUTH THIS TIME FOR DEGNITZ, POTTENSTEIN, GOSSWEINSTEIN, STREITBURG, FORCHEIM; BUT WAGNER'S THEMES PLAYED IN OUR MINDS.

In 1935
the idea of a visit to the U.S.S.R.
grew in my mind.

Frequently passing from London Bridge by Hay's Wharf,
& seeing the Soviet Boat in port, so local, & so inviting,
I asked "WHY NOT?"

"My boat is on the shore
And my bark is on the sea."

I then heard that my Northumbrian friends were also
proposing a visit, & sailing from Newcastle.

So with Byron's lines in mind I decided that this boat
should be my cradle for the 5 day sail from
London to Leningrad, & thence to Moscow.

"Adieu, Adieu! My native shore
Fades o'er the waters blue."

I had been thinking it was time to go East of Europe
& see for myself the changes which J. Gunter & E. Mannin
& so many others had written so much about.

"Cast wide the folding doorways of the East
For now is light increased!"
Francis Thompson

And so we hoped. Reading E. Fitzgerald, J.E. Flecker, F. Maclean,
I looked forward to visiting Central Asia, but that,
yes that had to wait for another 48 years

"Awake,! for Morning in the Bowl of Night
Has flung the Stone that puts the Stars to Flight:
And Lo! the Hunter of the East has caught
The Sultan's Turret in a Noose of Light."
from: Omar Khayyám; Ed. Fitzgerald.

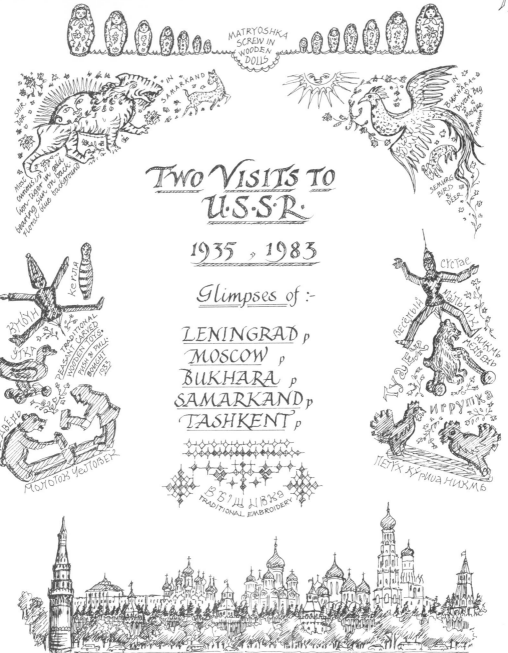

MATRYOSHKA
SCREW IN
WOODEN
DOLLS

IN SAMARKAND

SHIR DOR · MOST ominous is gold lion-tiger on back bearing sun on back · floruit glue background

IN BUKHARA · Divon Beg Mosque · tympanum · SEMURG BIRD & DEER

TWO VISITS TO U.S.S.R.

1935 , 1983

Glimpses of :-

LENINGRAD p
MOSCOW p
BUKHARA p
SAMARKAND p
TASHKENT p

КЕГЛА · ЗЯЧОЧН · УТКА · TRADITIONAL PEASANT CARVED WOODEN TOYS. PUSH & PULL BOUGHT 1933 · МЕДВЕДЬ · МОЛОТОВ ЧЕЛОВЕК

СУСТАЕ · ВЕСЁЛЫЙ МАЛЬЧИК · МАЛЬЧИКЪ МЕНЕДЬ · ТУЖЕЛЕ · ИГРУШКА · ПЕТУХ КУРИЦА НИХМЬ

ВВШ НВ кэ
TRADITIONAL EMBROIDERY

THE KREMLIN, SEEN FROM S· OF MOSCVA RIVER. BEYOND WALL TOWERS, SEE L· TO R·:- GRAND KREMLIN PALACE 1840, 9 GOLD CUPOLAS OF CATHEDRAL OF THE ANNUNCIATION ,1484 ; 5 SILVER CUPOLAS OF CATHEDRAL OF THE ARCHANGEL 1505; 5 GOLD CUPOLAS OF CATH OF THE ASSUMPTION [USPENSKY] 1475 ; IVAN THE GREAT BELL TOWER, 21 BELLS, 263', 329 STEPS, 1600.

[WORDS IN CYRILLIC CHARACTERS , USED DECORATIVELY IN THESE PAGES, ARE A SHOT IN THE DARK, PROBABLY INCORRECT]

LONDON (HAY'S WHARF) TO LENINGRAD & MOSCOW 1935

Joseph Paxton's splendid Crystal Palace Upper Norwood. From the family home near here, I started my journey.

26·7·35

BOARD SOVIET BOAT M·V·RUDZUTAR, & with some trepidation, considering:-

- '**O·G·P·U**' THE DREADED SECRET POLICE
- '**SIBERIA**' FATAL BANISHMENT
- '**KAPUT**' SIGNIFYING BROKEN DOWN NO USE

Such misgivings as these arose, but I dismissed them as the ship's siren sounded, the bascules rose & we slid away from the dear old Pool of London. Farewell to THE TOWER, THE MONUMENT, ST SWITHIN'S, THE MINT.

Farewell to Deptford [where I worked] to Greenwich Park [where I took daily picnics] to the Royal Naval College, to Inigo Jones' Queen's House. Goodbye all.

AS THEY FADED AWAY, & RUSSIA LAY AHEAD, I APPLIED MYSELF TO THE CYRILLIC ALPHABET & A USEFUL VOCABULARY.

A last look round, St. Swithin's etc. goodbye to David, & embark for Leningrad.

BIG BEN STRUCK AS I BOARDED

TOWER BRIDGE

THE TOWER OF LONDON

WHAT WOULD I FIND?
NO SOAP PROVIDED?
NO TOILET PAPER?
SEVERE SHORTAGES?
CROWDED TRANSPORT?
CAMERAS SUSPECT?
QUEUES, QUEUES.?
POSTPONED DATES?
DELAY, UNPUNCTUALITY?
LATE MEALS ETC?

5 DAY SAIL · N·Sea turbulent, meals untasted.

KIEL CANAL · A welcome haven. Eat, drink, with zest.

BALTIC SEA · a steady swell. Restful hours on deck, a holiday in itself. No cares. Good companionship. Lively young folk. Idealists. Many Americans. We talked Disarmament, Pacifism, World Peace, Utopia, Hay Diet, Yoga, Meditation, Contemplation.

QUEEN'S HSE & ROYAL NAVAL COLLEGE

ON BOARD:-
NO CLASS BARRIERS·
NO TIPPING·
NO LUXURIES·
ADEQUATE, GOOD,
FOOD & AMENITIES·
KIND ATTENTIONS·

This sail was a unique experience; a cameraderie of the whole personnel, crew & passengers alike. Each evening a free entertainment by the ship's crew in the theatre:- Russian Peasant, & Cossack Dancing, Balalaikas, Concertinas, Tambours, singing solo or in chorus. Willing passengers reciprocated with items.

CREW. A MUSICAL TRIO ON THE M.Y. RUDZUTAR

On the 5th day we scented land, heather sweet; spied it, then THE GULF. LENINGRAD 4·0 pm. RELUCTANTLY PASSPORTS HANDED IN, INTOURIST FOOD VOUCHERS DISTRIBUTED, CHECKED, COUNTED, POCKETED, & I SETTLED IN TO THE HOTEL EUROPE.

LENINGRAD'S LONG WATER FRONT ALONG THE RIVER NEVA

MOSCOW'S ASTONISHING ST· BASIL'S CATHEDRAL

Третьяковская галерея
картина

This sylph, this slim sprite of an acrobat delicately poised with split second timing on the moving ball, is the very essence of slender, spare grace.

'L'ACROBAT à la BOULE' Picasso 1905

'PASTORALES TAHITIENNES' Gauguin

The haunting mystery of Gauguin's figures, the placid and calm timelessness, whet the appetite for more. [See Tate Gauguins on team.]

Playful Pierrot & Harlequin solemn Mardi Gras CEZANNE 1881

Matisse "La Desserte" 1908

1935
I came to the U·S·S·R not only to hear about 5yr Plan achievements, & Stakhanovite records, but specially to enjoy the C19 French Paintings of Russian Collections; the Palaces with their famous rich interiors & fabulous array of treasures; the onion topped Cathedrals; chandeliers; icons; silver; jewellery; embroidery; tiled stoves; samovars; troikas; toys, & PEOPLE— & I was very richly rewarded.

'DANSEUSES' Degas

танцы

Poring over this exquisite pastel drawing I gloated, enjoying every nuance. made a meal of the colour, modelling, postures, & consummate use of chalk... As good as a visit to the Ballet itself!

арестанты

VAN GOGH'S compassionate expression of prisoners exercising in the walled yard.

суббота "SAMEDI" Derain

I like the quiet rectitude of these slender grey Victorian ladies, mistress, maid & slim hands of the embroideress. What long necks & wasp waists!

AS FROM
LENINGRAD 1983 ЛЕНИНГРАД
HERO CITY, & VENICE of the NORTH.

CURVE OF GENERAL STAFF H.Q.
TRIUMPHAL ALEXANDRIAN COLUMN, [OPP. WINTER PALACE; HERMITAGE]
CENTRAL IN VAST PALACE SQ:

This building is much more extensive than in this sketchy drawing

1812

OVER 2,000 soldiers handled this single granite monolith 47.5 metres [1834]

Dear M,

I am allowing myself the rare luxury of retrospect; 48 years back, & thought you might perhaps like to share it.

You'll recall that I arrived in LENINGRAD ahead of you, 9.7.35
You, my boon companion, & 3 friends, appeared later having travelled via Finland. Then together we 'rode' this Russian Adventure. We were young, ignorant, untravelled, impressionable. What an illuminating experience it was. Ernest spent the night in jail for photographing H.Q. O.G.P.U! [K.G.B]

ST. ISAAC'S CATHEDRAL
SEE THE VIEW FROM THIS DOME

ЗОЛОТОЙ

The "gleaming gold" dome raised high aloft is seen from far.

Needle spires & domes are land-marks above the wide level lines of this flat river city.

SPIRE OF THE ADMIRALTY

in Fountain Garden

PETER & PAUL CATHEDRAL 1703

Remember that coveted APPLE? We'd pined for fruit & eventually decided to blow the whole of 2/0³ on a single, sour, green apple!

The long romantic white nights were a joy. We danced till the small hours with never a blink of fatigue. We bathed in the Neva, & made friends with Dildarova.

But, oh! the Russian tardiness. What patience required! We waited for everything, for meals, 1st course, 2nd & 3rd. Remember those MENUS? 16 PACKED FOOLSCAP PAGES! Coaches could be hours late, taxis unpunctual, buses & trams full to bursting always hangers on. We often walked our way about [NO METRO THEN] crossing canal bridges, learning the map, sitting in Squares, making contact with the LOCALS.

КРАСИВЫЙ

Queues. Shortages. Seeing women labouring on men's jobs [road drills] shocked us. No unemployment, but folk looked down at heel.
STUCCO PEELING FROM ELEGANT STATELY BUILDINGS IN THIS C18 CITY OF PROSPECTS & PALACES, SQUARES, MONUMENTS, CANALS, BRIDGES, PARKS.
Built 1703, on swamp land. Forced labour; 40,000 men. Many died! Each cart entering the city must carry some stone. Nobility required to contribute by building noble Palaces, Mansions, Halls, in stone.

PETER THE GREAT. Bronze

OVER 600 [WATER] BRIDGES IN LENINGRAD
LOMONOSOV BRIDGE

A night sleeper train to MOSCOW gave a ten day break in our visit to LENINGRAD

KAZAN CATHEDRAL WITH CURVED COLONNADED WALK

WE VISITED THIS MUSEUM IN NEVSKY PROSPECT

To __MOSCOW__ by sleeper train. Stations seething with jostling travellers, all ages.
FOLK MIXED IN SLEEPERS; SEXES NOT SEPARATE. ARTHUR B. EMBARRASSED FINDING HIS BUNK!

Our Hotel, south of Moscva River gave good views of the Kremlin. St Basil's, astonishing
extravaganza, rose, an oasis in the wide desert of Red Square, so Russian, so fairy tale, so romantic.

How we enjoyed the Metro (in 1935). 14 Stations completed, each one palatial, individual &
spotlessly kept. We visited a Children's Village, a Collective Farm, Factories, Social
institutions, Bolshevo Open Prison, the Planetarium remember enthusiastic smocked Professor ?? All these very
serious. So our evening dancing, Theatres, Cinemas, Ballet etc made a welcome antidote.

The Kremlin was closed. Only the cupolas of Cathedrals & Bell Tower rose above the tall red
fish tail crenellated walls, guarded by 20 towers; Spasskaya Clock Tower the Big Ben of Moscow.

GUM [goom] in its great length was beseiged by crowds, like Selfridges. We explored back streets
seeking Old Moscow, ancient churches, the Tretyakoff etc. Much demolition, & now tower
blocks to house the homeless of this crowded city. How essential were the Parks of Rest &
Culture for these teeming flat dwellers. Wandering a Park before breakfast, we talked to 2
sweeping women [mime!] "Your husbands? Not married? Alone? Impossible!" they gasped incredulously.
IN 1935
WE ATE CAVIARE, RED & BLACK, STURGEON; CHICKEN IN VARIOUS PASTICHES; CUCUMBERS; SOUR CREAM; YOGURT, RYE BREAD ETC. VODKA, GREEN TEA.

Returning by sleeper to now familiar __Leningrad__ we braced ourselves to tackle at least
some rooms of the vast succession in the Hermitage Museum. 2 Visits. Remember Peacock clock beloved by children. ?
Dildarova & daughter joined us for a celebration farewell dinner, & next morning on the
station I waved Goodbye to you & our Newcastle friends. Ernest + camera once again retrieved by police.

THEN MY OWN SAGA BEGAN. Here is a reminder of it:-

TUESDAY
3.30pm Our hotel party packed luggage & assembled as instructed, to leave by coach for dock.
5.00pm The coach had not appeared. Excuses & confusion on their part, vexation on ours.
6.00pm We still waited & requested our passports, baffled by this frustrating delay.
7.00pm Passports produced for some of the party; exasperation & consternation for the rest.
8.00pm STATEMENT:- 'YOUR PASSPORTS ARE HELD AT EUROPA HOTEL', & thither we went by coach.
There passports distributed to all, bar 9 of us. Aggravation. "Yours will be at the dock".
But at the dock still no trace of the remaining passports! Unbridled indignation.

WHAT WAS THE REASON FOR THIS DISORGANISED CONFUSION, THIS CHAOS & DISRUPTION?
"LENINGRAD IS HOLDING A WORLD PHYSIOLOGICAL CONGRESS & IS SWAMPED BY THE INFLUX."
We hounded officials, remonstrated, agitated, & at last our passports were unearthed.
Inexcusable incompetence. But all was not yet plain sailing. For some, worse was to come!

<u>TUESDAY</u> CONTINUED

<u>10.0 pm</u>. Slow progress at Customs. We bought presents at the 'Torgsin' stall.

<u>11.0 pm</u> The wharf barrier closed!!!! Panic! We stranded passengers were told:- "BOAT NOW FULL". "MY BERTH IS THERE, BOOKED & PAID 3 MONTHS AGO!" "CAPTAIN'S ORDERS INVIOLATE" came the reply. "THEY'LL FLY YOU BACK"

Fly back like Ethel Mannin I thought. Rapturous joy. My cup was full.
[But E.F. American, panicked, & squeezing thro' a hole in barricades, stowed away.]

There were 7 of us. 2 persisted they'd not risk a flight in cranky Russian planes, & planned to catch the next boat in 4 day's time. 2 decided to make their slow way by train across Europe. Later we heard that the boat sailed at <u>2.0 a.m</u>, & WITH <u>12</u> UNOCCUPIED BERTHS! WHAT PREPOSTEROUS BUNGLING! SHAMEFUL!

<u>11.30 pm</u> So we remaining 7 returned to the hotel to secure an issue of vouchers, & beds.

<u>WEDNESDAY</u>
<u>9.00 am</u> A grim tussle with Travel Agent:- "A flight is £76! Too much! No hope!" HE WAS ADAMANT.
"You must boat or train" he declared. With dogged determination I insisted on a flight "The safety of my job depends on prompt return" I protested. He sparred. I fought. It was all most exhausting. "Call tomorrow," he said. So I resorted to Galleries, phoned Dildarova, joined her <u>10.0 pm</u> for coffee & Cinema, & there fell deeply asleep.

<u>THURSDAY</u>
<u>9. A.M.</u> Again approached Myers. He presented my Flight ticket! Conquest! Victory! Triumph! I'd won a gift from the wily Russians, £76 worth! I treasured the gift in my waistband sent an ecstatic card home, & gave myself up to relaxed enjoyment.

Evening dinner with Dildarova in her bed sitting room. She sometimes housed her daughter here also. "Small, but my own & private. With so many homeless, I'm lucky to have it." Her English was masterly, though little practised. Pre Revolution she'd travelled in Europe, a cultured aristocrat.

Now a humble manicurist & hairdresser, Dildarova enjoyed her free theatre pass. She wished to give me a token, & offered a manicure. What should I give her? My blouse? [blue celanese,] Delighted, she received it as if pure gold, infinitely grateful. <u>STRAPHANGING IN THE 1.0 am. BUS I RETURNED BLOUSELESS</u> — <u>BUT WEARING A MAC</u>.

<u>FRIDAY.</u>
<u>BUT MY TRAVEL SAGA IS NOT YET OVER</u>! 8.0 am. Car, Leningrad to Airport, a mere hut in open field. My whole being agog with excitement. We 3 weigh in. But who was the 4th? A portly giant of a man. American. Very queer speech. Exquisitely tailored. Palest grey suit; handkerchief, shirt, tie of silk; gold tie pin, cuff links & gold tip cane, leather gloves, sombrero, most handsome valises &

DOLL PRESENTS, BEDROOM, AND BASKET SLIPPERS

EDNA F. TERRIFIED AT THE THOUGHT OF FLYING
SQUEEZED THROUGH A HOLE

VOUCHERS FOR HOTEL MEALS & ROOM
INTOURIST SERVICE VOUCHERS

HARD BOILED TRAVEL AGENT
MYERS WAS EVENTUALLY PERSUADED TO ISSUE MY FLIGHT TICKET LENINGRAD-CROYDON

DILDAROVA GAVE ME MY FIRST MY EVER MANICURE I GAVE HER MY TURQUOISE BLOUSE.

ELMA (NASS) & TAJN (SEATTLE) ALSO RECEIVED FLIGHT TICKETS

<u>FRIDAY</u> *cont'd*
cabin trunk, very much overweight. My total luggage was merely a ruck sack &
compensated-[lucky him] How strange his speech! Curiously confused! WHO WAS HE?

10·0 A.M. Tiny plane for 4. Elma & Tain in front
stranger & me behind. Alas, storm ahead.
We waited. Suspense, apprehension. We rose.

Lightning played around us. The tiny
plane shuddered, bounced, swayed,
lifted sharply, dropped & rose in
turbulent motion. I turned yellow &
faint. My partner handed a cuspidor!

WE
4 PASSENGERS
THE FULL
COMPLEMENT.!

12·00 TALLINN. Safe landing – PRAISE BE! To hut café for lemon. Last to leave. WHOSE PASSPORT LYING
HERE ON THIS TABLE ??
Elma read:- "HENRY KENDAL THORR" she gasped " the notorious millionaire murderer of his wife's lover,
bought out of prison confinement! You <u>do</u> have risky companions, don't you?" she teased.
Handing the stray passport to our giant, we boarded a 'large' German plane. 18 passengers.
<u>MUCH RELIEF, & TOTAL CONFIDENCE IN THIS MONSTER</u> !

12·20 Five hops. <u>RIGA</u>, <u>KAUNAS</u>, <u>KONIGSBERG</u>, <u>DANZIG</u>, <u>BERLIN</u>. How keenly I watched the coastal map below!

17·00 ish. <u>BERLIN</u>. Now into a still larger Dutch Plane. 30 passengers plus steward. Luxurious! This
was flying in style, level, steady, a red setting sun, a golden rising harvest moon, turning
silver to reflect in the many waters of Amsterdam & Zuyder Zee. Was there any terra firma to land on?

22·00 ish <u>AMSTERDAM</u>. Now for the last hop across the Channel. I cabled home: "CROYDON AIR PORT·2330
PLEASE MEET ME" But alas, no one there. Deflation. I risked a pick up the few miles to Croydon
Rly STN & caught the last train home, coinciding with the arrival of the cable, THANKFUL FOR SAFE JOURNEY.

You & I promised ourselves to visit in 5 years time, but 48 years have elapsed. What changes we'll see
if we take up the challenge! Let's celebrate this year & include Bokhara & Samarkand. All good wishes, D.

JUNE 1983

Yes, infinite changes. Streets widened, redesigned, avenues lined with vast buildings, hotels, housing, trees.
Historic buildings restored. 'TORASIN' SHOPS, where foreign currency accepted, now called 'BERIOZKA'. Tower blocks ring
inner cities, where historic gold cupolas & spires, or blue domes & minarets insistently hold their sway &
weave their magic. The Cyrillic Alphabet may baffle, but why worry on the Metro
where each station can be identified by its own distinctive decorative style?

As one travels, history breathes. Names of invading races, of great
characters, of trades & craftsmanships etc flood the mind.
Such a history! Such achievements! So much beauty!
But the price paid in human suffering is not to be
forgotten!···3 crammed pages of selected notes follow tho'
drawings & enthusiasms would fill a whole book.

86

A FEW NOTES RE LENINGRAD & THEREABOUT

For the delights of water:- fountains, cascades, sprays, splashes, springs, plumes, surprise jets, [Peter's Pranks] & statuary, visit the seaboard gardens & parks of PETERHOF PALACES [now PETRODVORETS]

18 mls W. along Gulf.

In 1935, used as a Home of Rest, Water Cure treatment was prevalent. Then our visit was graced by a generous 7 course invitation lunch among these friendly & thriving patients.

We fought our way nobly through black caviare, sour cream, cucumber, sturgeon cutlets, sausage, salads, chicken & rice, cakes & sweets ices & green tea; then we met

Children of the Pioneer Camp

GRAND CASCADE
PETRODVORETS
AS I REMBER IT IN
1935.

Доброй день
очень приятно

shaved heads,
capped heads,
all jolly heads.

очень приятно
спасибо
досвидания

LACY CARVED
FASCIAS

First called 'Czarskoye Selo' [Czar's Village] then Detskoye Selo [children's Vill.] now PUSKIN after the poet. [15 mls S of Leningrad.]

We visited in 1935, & saw the proverbial extravagances & fantastic riches of Imperial Families in classic Palaces. Amazing! Rare marbles & woods mirror galleries, silks, candelabra, priceless gems, jewels beyond price, etc, etc. the cost never counted! See lady Londonderry's Diary 1837

Both Palaces occupied & ravaged by Germans 1941

CATHERINE'S PALACE GATES

Дворец ворота

PALACE SQUARE   LENINGRAD

THE VICTORY CHARIOT [1812] ABOVE GENERAL STAFF BUILDING ARCH; WITH WINGED FIGURE OF GLORY.

Chariots also on Narva Gate & Pushkin Theatre.

See also, impressive Victory Square 1941-2. [900day siege & bombardment of Leningrad Many thousands killed & starved to death.]

TAMING WILD HORSES EQUESTRIAN SCULPTURES ON ANICHKOV BRIDGE

IN LENINGRAD a succession of skyline figures crown parapets of the Winter Palace, the Admiralty, St Isaacs, & many more.

LOOK FOR GOLDEN GALLEON CAPPING THE NEEDLE SPIRE ADMIRALTY, LENINGRAD'

WATCHFULLY ATTENTIVE GRANDMA CUSTODIANS IN THE HERMITAGE GALLERY

женщины

THE LONG WATER FRONTAGE OF THE QUADRANGULAR WINTER PALACE [HERMITAGE]

IN MOSCOW A FEW NOTES

ALL HIGH CROSSES WELL ANCHORED

Cathedral of the ARCHANGEL 1509 silver 5 domes, shell hoods. Tsars were buried here. See tomb of Ivan the Terrible, 5 tier iconostasis, frescoes. See also 16th Assumption [Uspensky, Ivan throng] & other Kremlin churches

ST BASIL'S. ASTONISHING, UNBELIEVABLE, WHIMSICAL, REVELATION — & DOMES VARIOUSLY PATTERNED & COLOURED. WHAT

FANTASTIC EXUBERANCE! WHAT

WILD ABANDON, ZEST, WIZARDRY!

In 1935 the view from our bedroom window was across the Moscva River [no boats, up to the onion domes of St Basils Red [beautiful] Square. Few cars in the streets but trams crammed, trailing coupled & tripled
1935

AN EXTRAVAGANZA OF SHAPES JOSTLE & ELBOW EACH OTHER IN COSY PROXIMITY. A FAIRY TALE-A CHILD'S DREAM. EVERY DECORATIVE MOTIF PRESSED INTO SERVICE. RECKLESS DIVERSITY!!!

SAS

OGPU

SEE THE ICONOSTASIS IN EACH CATHEDRAL

gilded domes   CATHEDRAL OF ANNUNCIATION

Seen from high floor of Palace of Congresses during interval of Kirov Ballet. Fine stone portals. Polished Jasper agate floors. Icons [Greek Philosophers included in frescoed pillars & walls]

ICON VIRGIN OF VLADIMIR 1130 VIRGIN OF TENDERNESS

ICON OUR LADY OF TOLGA 1314

THIS ICON WAS BROUGHT TO MOSCOW TO ENCOURAGE TROOPS FIGHTING AGAINST TAMERLANE (15

In Iconography both seated & standing figures drawn same height. DEESIS, [prayer icons] show rows of saints.

THE KREMLIN, within its 1½ ml wall first opened to the public in 1955. Each wall tower of distinct design. Several visits are essential for the Cathedrals, Palaces, Museums & so on in this spacious citadel. [Another palatial attraction tho' underground is the Metro. [See Mayakovskaya & the Central Line.]

See the Red Square in evening emptiness to sense its spacious & vast spread. Under snow, the visionary splendour of coloured St Basils cupolas must look heraldic, rising from a white field.

What a contrast the severe low rectangular lines of the Lenin Mausoleum in polished red granite. Daily a long slow queue moves steadily past the bier.

Exquisite chandeliers of Palaces find their echo in some Metro stations.

1935
WHOLE DAY VISIT TO A COLLECTIVE FARM & WORKERS' HOMES, INCLUDING A RUSSIAN FARE 4 COURSE LUNCH Досвидания

VIEW FROM OUR BEDROOM WINDOW, HOTEL COSMOS 1983

553 ACRES OF THIS

SHOWING BUILDINGS OF ECONOMIC ACHIEVEMENTS EXHIBITION, 80 PAVILIONS OF DISPLAYS ETC, GARDENS & FOUNTAINS; T.V. TOWER 1967 WITH 7TH HEAVEN RESTAURANT; SPACE EXPLORATION MONUMENT; & DOME OF METRO STATION.

Крестьянин
Пожалуйста спасибо
Здравствуйте
Как вы поживаете

THE TRETYAKOV GALLERY OF RUSSIAN ART

WAS A NEAR NEIGHBOUR OF OURS IN 1935 See also:- HANDWORK MUSEUM, DECORATIVE FOLK ART MUSEUM, & OF COURSE THE PUSHKIN FINE ARTS MUSEUM & MANY MORE, HISTORICAL, LITERARY & SO ON.

DON'T MISS WIDESPREAD VIEW OF MOSCOW FROM THE LENIN HILLS, THE RIVER MOSCVA BELOW, & UNIVERSITY BEHIND YOU.

ISMAEL SAMANI TOMB C10

BUKHARA
UZBEKISTAN
A few slight notes.

ISMAIL SAMANI TOMB

I stood drawing in the dappled shadows of this ancient propped mulberry tree

The early monuments in unadorned brick work are to me spell binding. I stood transfixed & greatly moved by the perfection of this C10 architectural gem. Merely a dome on a cube, this mausoleum, built in humble brick, yet transcending all my conjectures, the bricks ingeniously conjured for inherent surface enrichment under all effects of light, in this background setting of parkland trees. Unique, exclusive.

Small composed serene, timeless. 4 sides alike. Bricks laid: on edge, upright, longways, cornerwise, concentric, feathered, notched, chequered. Amazing brickwork.

THE KALYAN MINARET C12 BRICK BUILT WITH 13 ORNAMENTAL BRICK BANDS

See from close below the perspectives of this superbly dominating & sturdy minaret 47 m. It served as a lighthouse for caravans of the steppe & desert, a watch tower against enemies, a platform for the call of Muezzin to prayer; & sadly a death tower [Mangid Dynasty] when criminals thrown from top

Stork's nests often seen on high points, encouraged by terminal spikes, on pylons, domes or minarets.

THE CITADEL. ANCIENT CITY FORTRESS; THE ARK. Parts are over 2,000 yrs old. In this flat city, it is built on an artificial hill. Today used as a museum

NO NAILS HERE IN BAZAAR ROOF

ARCADING OF MIRI ARAB MEDRESEH STILL IN USE

Beyond my drawing power in limited time.

GOLDSMITHS TRADING MARKET, LOOKING UP TO DOME & ALONG VAULTED STREET.

COLUMN CAPITAL PALACE ARK

"IT IS THE DUTY OF EVERY MAN AND WOMAN, MUSLIM, TO STRIVE AFTER KNOWLEDGE"

Older Muslims, bearded, wore the chupan turban, striped cotton coat & 'Russian' boots

SKULL CAPS
Silver on black for men

Colours on white, floral designs for women. Embroidered by hand. Worn toward back of head.

BLACK HAIR, BRAIDED INTO 12, OR 13 LONG THIN PLAITS TUBETEIKI, & JOLLY JAZZY STRIPED DRESSES.

PORCELAIN BOWLS, GREEN TEA & TALK, AD LIB

Seeking shadow, I welcomed the bubble domed street crossings of Merchants' Markets "TAJI", deeply intrigued by their arched beauty. So much skill expended to shelter mere trading centres; silks, cap makers, carpets, goldsmiths & so on.

How absurdly inadequate is a single page for Bukhara, a city teeming with interest. No room on it to draw the noble & substantial C15 C16 C17 Mosques. Such drawings & writings would fill a book.

SAMARKAND
ZERAVSHAN OASIS, UZBEKISTAN.

DOMES OF THE NECROPOLIS.
SHAKHI ZINDA

PAINTED MAJOLICA

ENTRANCE TO MAUSOLEUMS

FEATURES OF 3 SLENDER CORNER COLUMNS, INCISED GLAZE TERRA COTTA

A Jacob's ladder of high steps 35 of them then a long narrow street lined with blue domed, gaily tiled, finely coffered, delicately pilastered, buildings which house tombs of the Timurid Family friends & notables.

A unique, absorbing, & most moving sight, beyond imagining.
DON'T MISS THIS.

"The happiest, is the man who left the world before the world wanted him to go."

"A bird's strength is in his wings that of a man is in friendship"

STAR ORNAMENT OF MADRASAH OF ULUGH BEG, ASTRONOMER.

"Prayer, better than sleep";
Muslim Culture:
the Five Precepts of Islam;
Ornament, geometric floral or script';
Decoration in majolica, faience';
terra cotta;
all these & many more exercise the mind in this outdoor museum of Madrasahs, Mosques, & Mausoleums of Samarkand.

ULUGH BEG, PORTAL DECOR ... TILLYA-KARI PORTAL

KUFIC

NASHKI

THULTH

BANDS OF THESE 3 SCRIPTS CAN BE FOUND WOVEN WITH EACH OTHER, OR WITH FOLIAGE, ON COLOURED TILES OF BUILDINGS

WITH AMAZINGLY RICH & DASHING EFFECT. 2,3, COLOURS MOST FREELY & CLEVERLY INTERLACED

NOTE, TO REMIND OF ASTRONOMER 1394 - 1449 ULUGH BEG. PART OF HUGE SEXTANT

STALACTITE RIBS. DOME OF SHIR DOR MOSQUE.

THREE MADRASAHS [RELIGIOUS SCHOOLS] & MOSQUES IN REGISTAN SQUARE

The sheer impact of this architectural ensemble in brilliant sunlight, the blue domes, lacy faience enrichments, the monumental portals with deep black shadows, the sentinel minarets, make a breathless sight; noble; spacious, dignified, imposing, majestic.
THEY SAY "SEE NAPLES & DIE" I SUBSTITUTE REGISTAN SQ.

MADRASAH & MOSQUE OF ULUGH BEGH 1420

MOSQUE &

MADRASAH OF TILLYA KARI. 1618

MADRASAH & MOSQUE OF SHER DOR 1630

WEST

EAST

REGISTAN SQUARE
ANCIENT TRADING CENTRE

HOW THESE DRAWINGS NEED THE ESSENTIAL ELEMENT OF COLOUR - ORIENTAL! NO ROOM HERE FOR HIGHLY EXCITING DETAILS OF COLOURFUL MAJOLICA SURFACES.

Miles of travelling to & across comparatively small areas of this extensive, vast country [8½ million sq mls, 11 time zones] gave good variety:- Soviet boat, planes, train, metro, coach, taxi, bus, tram, hydrofoil, & 2 good legs [but never 4!]
[In 1935, flying time London to Leningrad 14 hrs; today 1983, 3½ hrs!]
The River boats & hydrofoils of today are an attraction to tourists

Clear views on the low flight, TASHKENT to BUKHARA [400 mls] Steppe, Sea of Tashkent, lakes, irrigations, mountains, deserts, drills, oil derricks etc. The Transcaspian train BUKHARA to SAMARKAND 180 mls [with friendly sleeper attendant, dispensing local wine БАЯН ШИПЕР, kvas, tomato, cuc,] gave a closer look at reclaimed land for cotton "white gold", fruit growing, Karakul sheep, goats etc.

Postage v.expensive here, travel v.cheap, Metros a joy to use, 5k. per journey. No litter, no vandalism, no unemployment. People friendly, helpful. Endless museums well attended, theatres & circus packed full. BUT, OH! THE TOILETS, & LACK OF THEM! OH! THE FLIES! BEWARE OF ICES, OF WATER. BOTTLED WATER RELIABLE?

Fanciful lively fountains splash generous water spouts in city squares, tho' in UZBEKISTAN "water is more precious than gold". Numerous memorials remind of conquests & great figures:- Avicenna, Ulug Beg, etc; Pushkin, Turgenev, Tolstoy, Gogol, Dostoyevsky, Chekhov, Stravinsky, Tchaikovsky, Rimsky Korsakov, Mussorgsky, Rachmaninov, Rubinstein, Borodin, Diaghilev, Nijinsky, Pavlova & so on.

<u>SOME MEMORIES:-</u>

The lilacs of Leningrad; wide treeshadowed streets of Tashkent & its beautiful Metro must be seen to be believed; the dry sweltering heat wave in Uzbekistan; [I slept naked & used my silk nightgowns as evening gowns!] sitting in a Mosque one still hot evening for the music & dance of swallows & Uzbeks; the social "double beds" spread with rugs for cross leg sitting & centred with low tables for green tea, kvas etc; the lively markets; the fringe of waist long black plaits & colourful silk susane dresses of young women; silver embroidered black caps of men; huge hair bows of children; the embossed copper workers in Mosque courtyard; the girls at gold embroidery; & the variety of superb buildings, are some among my unforgettable pleasures of these travels.
HOW COLOUR WOULD GIVE LOCAL CHARACTER TO ALL THESE DRAWINGS!

KHOKHLOMA WARE: TURNED WOOD, DECOR RED, GOLD, BLACK.

"BELOMORSKIYE UZORY", TURNED & CARVED WOOD

RUSSIAN BEAR, CARVED WOOD FROM BOGORODSKOYE.

БЕРЕЗКА
PORCELAIN COCK

PORCELAIN SAMOVAR FOR DOMESTIC USE

Peasant RAG DOLS КУКЛА ХРЕСТЬЯНКН

MATЬ PEBЁHOK КУКЛА ХРЕСТЬЯНКН

The only time I saw spectacles worn

VENDOR'S SAMOVAR.
LARGE, SUBSTANTIAL, FOR SELLING GREEN TEA.

КИМЁШЕ

GIRL EMBROIDERERS STITCH AWAY WITH SEQUINS & GOLD THREAD & BEADS ON THE TABLE FRAME: WAIST COATS, SLIPPERS, OR CAPS, BLOUSES, SMOCKS. ВЫШИВВА

THE CUSTOMARY "BEDSTEADS" SPREAD WITH CARPETS, CROSSED LEGS, GREEN TEA, CHINA BOWLS

[seen at our picnic under trees]

MY TINY (K·G·B·!) NOTE BOOKS & SKETCH PADS, HOLD MANY OTHER SCRIBBLINGS, BUT STRICT PAGE RATIONING EXCLUDES THEM.